Marketing Management
Information Systems

William R. King

University of Pittsburgh

MARKETING MANAGEMENT
INFORMATION SYSTEMS

PETROCELLI / CHARTER   NEW YORK 1977

First Printing

Printed in the United States of America

Library of Congress Cataloging in Publication Data

King, William Richard, 1938–
    Marketing management information systems.

    Includes index.
    1. Information storage and retrieval systems—
Marketing management.   I. Title.
Z699.5.M34K56   658.8   77-8219
ISBN 0-88405-394-6
ISBN 0-88405-444-6 pbk.

To Fay

Contents

Preface

The field of information systems is a rapidly growing one which has, in the past few years, come to consider marketing as one of the areas of greatest potential for the development of new varieties of management information systems. This represents a maturing of the field, which previously progressed, during the early years and decades after the advent of the computer, by giving primary emphasis to internally oriented accounting and financial information contexts. The marketing management information system (MMIS), with its emphasis on externally generated information about sales, customers, competition, and the environment, is therefore at the frontier of current information-system development in organizations.

This book is an attempt to address that area of applications in a way that makes it understandable to the marketing student and the practitioner. One objective of the book is to provide both the formally enrolled and independent student with an awareness of opportunities that exist in marketing for the application of information technology. A second objective is to provide some basic skills that the student can use to operate in the MMIS environment.

The book emphasizes the opportunities which exist for developing information systems that enhance the effectiveness of marketing organizations and improve the efficiency of their operation. These opportunities exist in a wide variety of public and private organizations that are emphasizing marketing to a greater degree than ever before.

The primary focus of the book is on the development of systems that will enhance the scope and quality of an organization's information collection and use. While there are many information system texts which emphasize the technical processes which may be used to develop cost-saving information systems, the true *management* information system is one which focuses on *improved managerial decision support*. Usually, this is not accomplished through a cost-saving approach of eliminating clerks and manual procedures. Rather, it is to be accomplished by providing managers with information that will permit them to make better decisions and to take advantage of opportunities of which they might otherwise be unaware.

The book contains exercises for class discussion at the end of each chapter which are meant to be thought provoking; they are not meant to be definitive tests of the degree to which text material can be regurgitated.

Another feature of the book are the group projects, which appear in the appendix. These can serve as devices for applying the text material and for extending understanding through confronting realistic situations in the application of academic ideas.

As in any writing effort, many people deserve the author's thanks for help, both direct and indirect, with the conception and development of the book. Those whose contribution was major and direct deserve special recognition—the series editor, Professor Leonard L. Berry of Georgia State University, who first suggested that I undertake the effort; Professor David I. Cleland of the University of Pittsburgh, my longtime colleague and friend, whose ideas have become so intertwined with my own that he may find much of himself in this book; Carol Capone and Pamela Reinhard, who typed various versions of the manuscript and whose efforts were above and beyond the call of duty; my family and especially my wife Fay, to whom the book is dedicated and without whom it and much else would never have been done.

William R. King

1

Marketing Management Information Systems

The term *marketing management information system* can best be understood by examining its constituent elements. This introductory chapter briefly considers the operational meaning and significance of each of the words which make up the term MMIS and combinations of these words, such as *management information systems.*

Defining MMIS by its Constituent Parts

This process of defining terms, although sometimes tedious, is a necessary antecedent of good communications. The difficulties encountered when words, however common they may be, are not clearly defined is well illustrated by Ackoff's description of a conversation about the implicit definition of the word *room* which had been used in gathering survey data.

The survey had been conducted without an explicit definition of "room." He met with the designers of the survey and asked what definition they had used implicitly. They were impatient with the question, observing, "Everyone knows what a room is." The author persisted, and one of those present offered: "A room is a space enclosed by four walls, a floor, and a ceiling." The conversation then proceeded much as follows:

The author asked, "Can't a room be triangular?"

"Sure. It can have three or four walls."

"What about a circular room?"

"Well, it can have one or more walls."

"What about a paper carton?"

"A room has to be large enough for human occupancy."

"What about a closet?"

"It must be used for normal living purposes."

"What are 'normal living purposes'?"

"Look, we don't have to go through this nonsense; our results are good enough for our purposes."

"What were your purposes?"

"To get an index of living conditions by finding the number of persons per room in dwelling units."

"Doesn't the size of the room matter?"

"Yes, we probably should have used 'square feet' of floor space, but that would have been too hard to get."

"Doesn't the height of the room matter?"

"I guess so. Ideally, we should have used volume."

"Would a room with 10 square feet of floor area and 60 feet high be the same as one with 60 square feet of floor area and 10 feet high?"

"Look, the index is good enough for people who use it."

"What do they use it for?"

"I'm not sure, but we've had no complaints." [1]

Marketing

Marketing is that function of organizations, both private and public, which is concerned with all decisions and activities involved in the planning and execution of operations that supply goods and services to fulfill consumer needs. The *consumer* who is served by marketing in this definition includes individuals, groups, and organizations other than just the traditional users of *consumer products*. For instance, industrial firms are consumers of office supplies and machine tools as well as of electrical power and public "goods" such as highways and police protection. Families and communities are consumers of government flood-relief programs after disasters occur, and scientists working in research laboratories are consumers of scientific and technical information during the normal course of their activities.

The field of marketing is therefore concerned with the myriad *institutions*—manufacturers, wholesalers, retailers, government agencies, transportation companies, etc.—and the *processes*—advertising, personal sales, distribution, etc.—by which goods, services, information, knowledge, and any other things [2] are directed toward the fulfillment of needs. Thus, whether the marketing objective is to sell toothpaste or to enhance the general quality of life through effective antilittering programs, the field of marketing is broadly concerned with improving conditions by fulfilling needs.

Management

Management is the process by which choices are made and actions are taken. Put simply, management is the process of deciding and doing in any situation.

However, in a modern world which is increasingly dependent on large organizations, the most significant situations are those which require *organizational management;* deciding and doing in a context which is characterized by *organized group activity* and *objectives* toward which the group effort is directed.

These objectives are pursued by managers, who make decisions concerning *desired objectives* and concerning *relationships among resources*—the people, money, machines, and material which can be employed to seek those objectives. Managers then see that their decisions are carried out and that they have the

---

[1] R. L. Ackoff, *Scientific Method: Optimizing Applied Research Decisions* (New York: Wiley, 1962), pp. 147–148. Quoted with permission.

[2] In the remainder of the book, we shall often use the term *product*. However, it should be remembered that the *product* may be a service or information as well as the physical entity that most of us think of when the term is used.

desired effect. When necessary, they use *control actions* to redirect their resources toward the desired objectives.[3] Since managers of large organizations cannot literally do each and every thing that is required as a result of the decisions that they make, organizational management is a process of *working through others* to achieve broad organizational objectives, such as profit or social welfare, or specific objectives, such as the development of a successful new product or the efficient construction of a building.

Management may be thought of as involving two major elements, planning and control. *Planning* involves decisions and actions concerning the *future* of the organization: What business should we be in? What kinds of people will we need to be effective in the 1980s? What impact will increased leisure time have on the utilization of our products?

Control involves decisions and actions related to the *present* organization: How can we schedule production to achieve the minimum machine down time? Which people should be assigned to which tasks? How many TV ads do we need?

Every manager is involved to some degree in both planning and control, but the jobs of many managers emphasize the control element. Indeed, this is so even in many jobs which have the word *planning* in their title. The job of a production planning manager, for example, is largely control oriented, in that it emphasizes the present and the immediate future rather than the longer-range future, which is an intrinsic aspect of true planning.

Marketing management

Marketing managers make decisions concerning products and services to be offered by their organizations, prices to be charged, advertising and sales appeals to be used, funds to be allocated to various promotional media and campaigns, personal sales effort to be expended, and a wide variety of other marketing variables which form a part of overall organizational management.

Despite the fact that marketing managers limit their concern to marketing decision variables, and without engaging in a fruitless discussion of the relative importance of marketing functions compared with other organizational functions such as production and finance, it should be pointed out that *marketing decisions tend to be intrinsically involved in most of the strategic choices of the organization.* Indeed, strategic planning is often thought of in futuristic product-market terms—Which products or services should be distributed to which markets or market segments?—and product and market choices are intrinsically marketing

[3] This operational definition of management, stated in terms of observations that could be made if certain operations were to be performed, is adapted from D. I. Cleland and William R. King, *Management: A Systems Approach* (New York: McGraw-Hill, 1972), chap. 1.

decisions.[4] Thus, while marketing is indeed only one of the variety of functions that must be performed if the organization is to prosper, it is the one function which most vitally affects the organization's future because future success is primarily dependent on new generations of products and on developing markets which the organization does not already exploit.

Of course, marketing management is equally important in determining the organization's present performance. As the old marketing cliché says, everything is cost until the product is sold.

One can, therefore, readily identify the great importance of marketing to every person, group, or organization that has needs to be fulfilled; marketing is the function through which the organizations of our society work directly to fulfill those needs. At the level of the individual organization, the same importance is manifested, since the marketing manager's controllable variables are those which significantly and directly determine both the present performance and future prospects of the organization.

Information

Information is a concept familiar to everyone; yet the use of the word in the term MMIS is somewhat more precise than its common use. Information consists of *evaluated data,* data being symbols, usually numbers, used to represent things. For instance, the sequence of digits 213–4318 represent data. However, when one is told that these seven digits represent the phone number of an attractive member of the opposite sex who is anxiously awaiting a call from you, these data are transformed into information. *The data have been evaluated for use in a specific context and have thereby become information.*

Information is of central importance to good management. Indeed, virtually everyone would agree that the quality of the available information largely determines the quality of decisions which people are able to make. If one is choosing a new car or a spouse, he wants to have as much information as possible about the alternatives which are available so that he is able to predict the consequences of the choice. If the available information suggests that the car under consideration may not get good gas mileage or that the prospective spouse may demand to be served breakfast in bed each morning, the rational person will wish to take this information into account in making a decision.

Management information

The manager is particularly concerned with having complete and high quality information available since the job of planning and controlling the organization's

[4] For instance, see H. I. Ansoff, *Corporate Strategy* (New York: McGraw-Hill), 1965.

activities intrinsically involves a steady stream of complex choice situations: which person to promote, which product to market, how much to spend on advertising. If managers can make *informed choices* based on *relevant information,* they are more likely to experience good results and to move toward the achievement of the goals of the organization.

The nature of present-day management is such that the need for information is crucial and well recognized. Managers must deal with complex phenomena that are not easily understood: When today's teenagers begin to marry and form families, what product characteristics will be most attractive to them? What will be the effect on sales of a contemplated price increase? How high can the price be raised before profits are negatively affected? These issues and many others are the day-to-day grist of marketing management and all can be answered intelligently only on the basis of relevant information: the present product preferences of teenagers, trends in consumer expectations and spending patterns, and price elasticities. All of this is *management information* if it is related to a decision problem faced by managers in planning for or controlling their organization's activities.

Marketing management information

The nature of the information needed to manage the marketing function of an enterprise is unique because of its diversity. While the basic *need* for information is the same for the marketing manager as for any other manager, the marketing manager is faced with a vast array of data of differing varieties, differing forms, and differing degrees of credibility.

Another unique feature of marketing information is that *it is largely generated outside the organization.* The accountant, production manager, personnel manager and many others within the organization deal primarily with information that is generated internally, from the firm's own production facilities, employees, etc. However, marketing information is largely generated in the external environment—from customers, potential customers, untapped market segments, competitors, government regulators, etc. The source of marketing information is, more so than in any other functional area of the organization, the organization's *external environment.*

Marketing information is also diverse in its form and substance. One important variety of marketing information is derived from data on consumer *expectations, attitudes, needs,* and *intentions.* The information created from such data is the basis for implementing the *marketing concept* of developing products and services to fulfill needs. However, such data are much less objective and well defined than are data on costs, production quantities, interest rates, etc. These *attitudinal data* reflect *human perceptions* rather than physical phenomena.

For instance, Table 1-1 shows the results of interviews conducted by Ogilvy

TABLE 1-1 Planning to Give as Christmas Gifts

	Total	Men	Women
Clothing	39%	34%	43%
Toys	15%	16%	13%
Cash	12%	19%	5%
Homemade items	10%	3%	17%
Home furnishings	6%	2%	9%
Food gifts	4%	3%	4%

and Mather [5] concerning the intentions of the public toward the purchase of Christmas gifts. These data, coupled with other results which show consumer intentions to spend less, to purchase gifts for fewer people, and to give different kinds of gifts from those they had given previously, provide valuable guides for the development of effective marketing strategy and promotional tactics.

While some data about purchase intentions (such as those of Table 1-1) provide only general guidance to decision making, other such subjective data may be so directly related to marketing decisions as to clearly constitute marketing *management* information. For instance, the data of Table 1-2 describe specific consumer intentions with respect to the purchase of their next car.[6] The implications of Table 1-2 for the development of new smaller-sized cars and other marketing programs for autos should be rather clear-cut.

Of course, this is not to say that all marketing information is subjective and attitudinal in nature. Marketing information also includes some objective data, but even that is often of a variety which requires unique data collection processes in the external environment. For instance, *product purchase and usage data* are basic to the understanding of how, why, and with what frequency consumers use products and services. Such data are usually obtainable through *panels*—groups of consumers who record their purchases and/or usage of various products on a continuing basis. Such panels must be specifically established, administered, and compensated in order to obtain basic purchase and usage data since records of retail sales do not reflect either the purchase or usage behavior of individuals.

In the realm of industrial products, the need for specialized data collection processes is no less severe. For instance, producers of central air conditioners would not normally be aware of the *end use* to which their products were put. Transaction records would routinely show only that a sale had been made to X YZ Construction Co., but they would not show whether the unit was installed in a

[5] Taken with permission from "Operation Listening Post," Issue No. 4, Ogilvy and Mather, New York.

[6] Taken with permission from "Operation Listening Post," Issue No. 4, Ogilvy and Mather, New York.

TABLE 1-2

Next Car Compared to Present		Next Car Size	
Smaller	27%	Subcompact	15%
Same size	58%	Compact	25%
Larger	5%	Intermediate	21%
		Full size	26%

hospital, apartment building, bowling alley, or any of the other myriad uses for which it is feasible. Yet, for marketers to assess the potential of their business, they must have basic information on the current uses to which their product is put. To do so may require either a special survey of customers, since they are largely intermediaries rather than final users, or the establishment of a routine system for inquiring as to the end use at the time of sale and recording and processing these data which are necessary only for purposes of marketing planning.

Another consideration which comes into play in marketing information has to do with its *reliability* and *credibility*. Do the attitudes, expectations, and intentions which survey respondents report really reflect their underlying thoughts and beliefs? Is the respondent motivated to "look good" or to appear to be sophisticated in responding to an attitudinal survey? Do panel members neglect to report everything that should be reported about their purchase and usage of products? Do some of the respondents in a phone survey give an "easy answer" about product end use rather than go to the trouble of searching out the particular end use in their records? The answers to all these questions about the reliability and credibility of marketing information is: "Probably Yes." Such data have inherent properties which make them less credible and reliable than data which reflect physical counts.

Indeed, the implications of this may sometimes be severe. The data of Table 1-2, collected in May 1975, reflect a clear trend toward preferences for smaller autos. Yet by 1976, sales of full-sized cars were surging and auto companies found it necessary to offer cash rebates on subcompact and compact cars, as they had been doing on full-sized models only slightly more than a year earlier.

This reflects a degree of changeability on the part of consumer attitudes which may be totally at odds with time lags inherent in choices that must be made by marketing managers. This was the case in late 1976 when General Motors introduced entirely new, scaled down, full-sized models at a time when large cars were at the peak of their sales resurgence. The decision made by GM was, of course, dictated by additional considerations that went beyond consumer attitudes like those reflected in Table 1-2; but the message to wise marketers is clear. They must be aware of the inherent unreliability of their data as well as of the fickle nature of the consumer. If they are so aware, they may take steps to account for this and, therefore, be able to make use of the data despite the fact that they are not as objective as the data which support decision making in other areas of the enterprise.[7]

One of the critical characteristics of marketing management information is its complexity and the complex nature of the relationship between the information and the managerial action which the information is to support. This is well illustrated by an information gathering activity known as the Laboratory Test Market (LTM),[8] which provides a method of simulating the test marketing of a product. The LTM involves an experimental supermarket where products are sold to customers on a controlled basis after they have viewed advertisements and other promotional materials concerning products which are being evaluated. Subjects are interviewed as to their attitudes and follow-up interviews are made at appropriate intervals.

This simulation provides the marketer of a potential new product with the following information: [9]

An estimate of potential market share/volume.

Measure of the trial generating power of the brand.

The dynamics of the market for the product field in terms of:
Various market segments and their relative size.
Particular issues that dominate consumer behavior and attitudes in the product field.
Current brand preferences.

The response of the market to the proposed new product in terms of the factors stimulating trial:
Advertising
Package
Price.

An in-depth understanding of the attitudinal and behavioral factors that have generated trial.

The characteristics of consumers who try the new product:
Demographically
Attitudinally
Behaviorally.

An understanding of how the product performs under normal, at-home conditions in the context of expectations.

Actual in-home use patterns: who, when, how, how often.

---

[7] For instance, see David M. Stander, "Testing New Product Ideas in an 'Archie Bunker' World," *Marketing News*, 15 November 1973, pp. 1, 4.

[8] The Laboratory Test Market is a commercial activity of Yankelovich, Skelly, and White, Inc.

[9] "Laboratory Test Market," Publication of Yankelovich, Skelly, and White, Inc., New York, April 1976, pp. 2–3. Quoted with permission.

Repurchase and reasons for the repeat decision.

Comparisons of the new product against competitive products.

One can readily see the relevance and value of this information to a firm considering the marketing of a new product. However, there is a complex relationship between these items of information and the variety of choices which the marketer must make about the price, promotion, and packaging of a new product. The manager must understand these relationships if he is to use the information intelligently. Otherwise, the rich store of data provided by such simulations as LTM cannot really be called marketing management information.

One, and only one, of the dimensions of this complex relationship is the uncertainty which is inherent in the information. If this is understood, it presents little problem; if it is not, poor decisions may be made on the basis of sophisticated information. For instance, David Sculley, a marketing manager for H.J. Heinz has been quoted on the subject of using Sales Waves, another commercially available information service.[10]

> Purchase frequency is generated directly from Sales Wave data. I should point out, however, that our real marketplace experience suggests that the purchase frequency provided by Sales Waves overstates the real life figure by 20–25 percent.[11]

In addition to assessing the uncertainty in the Sales Wave information, Mr. Sculley goes on to relate the information to the way in which it is used in the decision process.

> We want to know as early in the development process as possible whether a particular project represents a worthwhile business opportunity. Why go farther than six months on a project that could be weeded out early?
>
> Conversely if a product appears to be $20 million plus in volume potential, why not rearrange internal priorities to put maximum effort behind it?[12]

Thus, Heinz recognizes the uncertainty in the information and uses it in a way that guides their choices, while taking the high uncertainty into account. They thereby convert what some might believe to be highly inaccurate data into valuable marketing management information.

Systems

The term *systems* is much used and much misunderstood. A dictionary style definition of a system would be "an assemblage of interrelated and interdependent

---

[10] Sales Waves is a service of Data Development Corporation, New York, which provides estimates of the sales potential of a product as well as an understanding of the reasons for purchase and non-purchase.

[11] As quoted in "New Product Forecasting Techniques May Make Test Markets Obsolete," *Marketing News,* American Marketing Association, 19 November 1976, p. 3.

[12] Ibid.

elements forming a unified whole." Thus, just about anything can be thought of as a system—things typically referred to as such (the nervous system, being a collection of cells, neurons, and the like which form a unified whole) and those which are not (a product system, being a collection of related products and services sold as a package).

The critical elements of the definition are the terms *interrelated* and *interdependent*. If the elements that one is considering are not interrelated or interdependent, they may still be thought of as a system, but *there is no particular advantage in doing so*. Interrelated elements affect each other; interdependent ones depend on each other. Therefore, considering a set of interrelated and interdependent elements as an overall system, rather than considering each individually, provides a richer basis for understanding.

For instance, one could not readily understand the solar system by looking at the separate behavior of the planets, moons, and other bodies which make it up. The various parts affect and depend on one another to such a great degree that the existence of the planet Pluto was known before it was actually ever observed. The relationships among the other bodies was such that *Pluto had to be there* even if it could not be seen. When more powerful telescopes became available, it was eventually viewed by the astronomers who knew it was there all the while.

So too with the relationships among many of the things with which managers deal. A factory must be viewed as a system of interrelated parts rather than as a collection of individual machines if one is to understand the need for in-process inventories—those partially completed items that are stored between sequential work centers to make sure that variations in processing speed and in different job assignments to machines will not result in excessive lost time. The marketing system must also be viewed as a system if one is to comprehend the complex relationships between product design, packaging, price, and promotional strategies as they affect sales.

Even the overall organization must be viewed as a system in order to understand how overall goals require trade-offs among the conflicting objectives of various departments and people in the organization. For instance, consider the corporate viewpoint involved in the simple decision concerning what products are to be produced and in what quantities.[13] The production department of the enterprise would undoubtedly prefer that few products be produced in rather large quantities so that the number of costly machine setups needed to convert from production of one product to production of another are minimized. Such a policy would lead to large inventories of a few products. Sales personnel, on the other hand, desire many different products in inventory so that they can promise early delivery on any product. Financial managers recognize that large inventories tie up money which could be invested elsewhere—hence, they want low total

[13] This illustration is adapted from a similar one by the author in "The Systems Concept in Management," *Journal of Industrial Engineering,* May 1967, pp. 320–321.

inventories. Personnel managers desire constant production levels so that they will not constantly be hiring new workers for short periods of peak production and laying them off in slack periods. One could go on to identify objectives of almost every functional unit of an organization relative to this simple tactical decision problem. As demonstrated, these objectives each conflict to some greater or lesser degree: low inventory levels versus high inventories, production of many products versus production of only a few products, and so forth.

The same situation can exist at every other level of the enterprise. The production department must constantly balance the speed of production with the proportion of rejects and the proportion of defective products which are not detected. The marketing function becomes involved when defective products cause complaints and lost sales. Indeed, wherever the labor has been divided in an organization, the management task of effectively integrating the various elements is paramount, and this can be effectively accomplished only if responsible managers adopt the systems approach to the system which is their domain.

The systems concept or viewpoint is the simple recognition that any organization is a system which is made up of segments, each of which has its parochial goals. Recognizing this, one can set out to achieve the overall objectives of the organization only by viewing the entire system and seeking to understand and measure the interrelationships, and to integrate them in a fashion which enables the organization to pursue its overall strategic goals effectively.

Management systems

The systems view may be applied to just about any complex of interrelated and interdependent items. As such, it forms a valuable perspective for understanding and managing organizations.

However, there are many elements of organizations which are themselves referred to as systems, for example the production system, the personnel system, and the compensation system. This use of the term *system* is familiar to all when it refers to an existing set of interrelated procedures, policies, and ways of doing things which have been institutionalized to accomplish a given objective, be it the production of goods, the administration of human resources, or the payment of compensation to employees.

Many of the existing systems in an organization are *management systems*— those that have been developed to facilitate the management process in the organization. Management systems are complex assemblages of such things as procedures, reports, models, and information which prescribe the way in which some aspect of the organization is to be managed. For instance, a *strategic planning management system* might incorporate a format for the plan, prescribed plan content, a planning process with schedules, task assignments in the planning process, the specification of informational inputs to planning, etc. A *management control system* would encompass similar elements which are addressed to achieving good allocation and control of resources in the organization.[14]

Information systems

One variety of a system which is found in every organization is the *information system*—the assemblage of data, reports, typewriters, computers, programs, procedures, people, and other entities which have to do with the collection, analysis, and dissemination of information in the organization.

Normally, an information system conjures up the image of computers with flashing lights and whirling tapes; but every organization has an information system, whether or not it possesses these sophisticated appurtenances. An organization may well use file cabinets rather than magnetic tapes to store data and it may use a pocket calculator or abacus rather than electronic computers to calculate. Nonetheless, it has an information system since data are collected, translated into useful information, processed, and disseminated.

Information systems are pervasive in modern society. The Internal Revenue Service has a data bank which includes all taxpaying Americans and, one might suspect, some non-taxpaying ones as well. The public library has an *information retrieval system* which can produce a copy of past newspaper articles on a specified subject within a few moments. Even the corner grocery store has records, invoices, tax returns and other documents filed in a manner which facilitates their retrieval and use. Moreover, even such a small organization has established procedures for routine retrieval at regular intervals such as when accounts are due.

Management information systems

A management information system is both a *management system* and an *information system*. Thus, unlike data bank information systems or information retrieval systems, where the system's capabilities for providing information may be an end in itself, *the management information system (MIS) is a variety of information system which is specifically designed to support management decision making and action.* Thus, while it is necessary for a bank to compile information on customers' balances in order to operate, the system which it uses to store and to retrieve such data is not necessarily an MIS. If such data are not used by managers in making decisions and taking action, the data are not really information and the system is a *data system* (or sometimes confusingly called an "information system"), but it is not a *management information system.*

---

[14] For an outline of various kinds of management systems, see P. P. Shroderbeck (ed.), *Management Systems: A Book of Readings* (New York: Wiley, 1967).

This distinction is not completely rigorous and valid since obviously some data can be used for management purposes as well as other purposes. The distinction is useful, however, to counter the recent confusing trend toward removing Data Processing Department signs from the doors of computer rooms and replacing them with signs reading Management Information Systems Department. An MIS is not just a computer system; it is *an information system specifically designed to support the management function in the organization.* Other organizational information systems support other functions, for example, the processing of transactions such as the payment of invoices and the shipment of goods.

Marketing management information systems

After defining each of the constituent words and several compound phrases, we can see that the MMIS is that organizational information system which directly supports *marketing* management decision and actions. While such a system can be designed and developed to encompass transaction processing as well, it warrants the title MMIS only insofar as it provides information which is meant to improve management *effectiveness* in the organization. The many information systems which are designed only to improve *efficiency* (e.g., to replace clerical data processing) are not true MMISs even though they may involve solely the marketing function.

The MMIS and Other Organizational Information Systems

Despite the importance of the marketing function, it is only one of many functions which are performed by most organizations. Each of these functions, production, accounting, finance, etc., must be managed and each requires that managers be provided with good information if good performance is to be expected.

Much of the information needed for the sound management of these various functions is based on the same data. For instance, order information required by the production department to determine which products to schedule for production and in which sizes and colors is also required by marketing to determine which products are the most successful and, therefore, which to advertise and promote most heavily. The financial department needs similar information from orders to determine working capital requirements.

Thus, a valid conceptual model for an overall organizational information system might look like that in Figure 1-1, which shows a common *data base* being drawn on by many different organizational functions and departments.

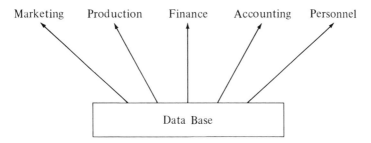

Marketing   Production   Finance   Accounting   Personnel

Data Base

FIGURE 1-1 Integrated Data Base

Why MMIS rather than MIS?

If the conceptual model of Figure 1-1 is valid, the need to separate the marketing management information system from the overall organizational information system comes into question. If there is to be a common data base with multiple uses, why not just think of it all as one system and construct it that way? Indeed, isn't that precisely the value to systems thinking? And, aren't there even more elements of an overall information system that might be used in common by many different departments and functions?

The answers to these questions must basically be positive. Figure 1-1 does represent the *ideal* conceptual model for an organizational management information system (MIS). However, this does not imply that it is *practical* to implement this model, nor indeed that it *should* be done this way.

Most large organizations that have tried to implement the *integrated data base* depicted in Figure 1-1 have found the concept to be difficult to bring to reality. There are many reasons for this among which are the vast size of the data base, the diversity of data (e.g., some numerical and some alphabetical), and the difficulty in assuring that data are put into the data base in forms which will be useful by *all* functions.

Modular system development

Of course, the concept of an overall MIS built on a common data base and serving all organizational functions also does not necessarily imply that the development of the entire system should be undertaken all at once. Again, it is often not feasible even to think about the myriad relationships and needs for information in an organization as a whole. Practically speaking, one must think in terms of organizational subunits to make the systems design and development problems manageable.

This approach to systems design is often referred to as a *modular* approach—

developing system modules and then tying them together to form an overall system.

This modular approach is the most commonly used in systems design because it has proved *practical* and effective at the same time. If system modules are developed in terms of an overall plan and with the recognition that each must eventually be integrated with other modules, the overall concept of Figure 1-1 can be achieved or at least approximated.

Functionally defined modules (a marketing module, a production module, etc.) are, therefore, natural for the organization to consider, since this is the way in which the organization itself is most often defined. Thus, the MMIS concepts to be discussed here may be thought of as directed solely toward the development of an MMIS or toward the development of an MMIS module of an overall organizational information system. In some cases, the former will be more appropriate, as with an organization whose principal activity is marketing; in other cases, the latter will correspond more realistically with the organization's overall system development plans. In either instance, the principles and techniques to be developed in this book are appropriate.

Hierarchical Levels of the MMIS

An MMIS may be thought of as having four distinct hierarchical levels of activity as described in Figure 1-2. These levels are depicted in the shape of a pyramid to suggest the typical magnitude and volume of activity at each level.

FIGURE 1-2 Hierarchical levels of the MMIS

Strategic Planning

Management Control

Operational Control

Transaction Processing

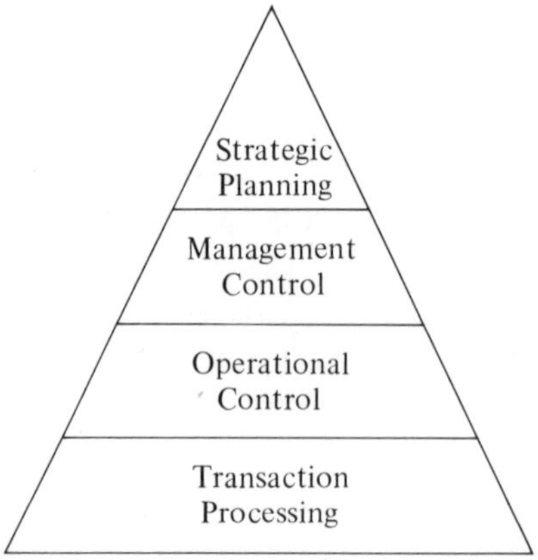

Transaction processing

The lowest level of the pyramid, transaction processing, involves the highest volume of activity. Transactions such as ordering, shipment, and invoicing are the basic administrative and informational work of the organization. Every item that is sold, removed from inventory, passed on to the next stage in the production process, shipped or placed in inventory represents a basic transaction. Every person that is hired, loan that is made, or payment that is received similarly represents an organizational transaction that is recorded on paper (or computer tapes or some record-keeping medium), operated on in various ways, such as invoice amounts being summed to determine total sales, and then filed away to become apart of the operating history of the organization.

Operational control

At the level of operational control,[15] information is processed to make sure specific tasks are carried out efficiently and effectively. The emphasis is still on individual transactions at this level, but it is on *controlling* these transactions, ensuring that they get done properly and efficiently, rather than focusing on the actual performance of the transactions.

For instance, the matching of order and shipment transaction records to ensure that orders are processed is a simple element of operational control. So too is the more complex process of recomputing current stock levels to reflect the impact of a recent shipment and the subsequent matching of the newly computed stock level against a reorder point level to determine if a new supply of stock is needed. The updating of the status of an in-process order is also an operational control activity.

Since most of these operational control-level activities are associated with individual transactions, their total volume is quite large. This is reflected in Figure 1-2, which shows them just above the level of transaction processing.

Management control

At the management control level of the pyramid, information is consolidated to ensure, *in the aggregate,* that resources are employed effectively and efficiently. At this level, information is necessary by customer, by cost center, or by department rather than by individual transaction. Thus, the pyramid of Figure 1-2 narrows in terms of the relative volume of activity.

---

[15] The taxonomy of operational control, management control, and strategic planning as the three integrated functions of management is widely accepted and adapted from R. N. Anthony, J. Dearden, and R. F. Vancil, *Management Control Systems,* (Homewood, Ill.: Irwin, 1965).

Management control activities are illustrated by the monthly comparison of the actual expenses of a department with the amounts previously budgeted for various expense categories and the recomputation of the time required to complete a project on the basis of data reflecting progress to date.

Strategic planning

At the highest level, strategic planning, the pyramid is narrowest, indicating a relatively low volume of activity. Strategic planning is concerned with establishing organizational objectives and strategies and the alignments of resources which will be used to achieve the objectives. Thus, strategic planning decisions affect the physical, financial, and organizational framework within which the organization's activities are performed.

Examples of strategic planning activities are the establishment of earnings-per-share objectives, the determination that a firm will seek to achieve its goals through the introduction of new products, and the decision to allocate a million dollars to new product-development projects.

Management information at the various hierarchical levels

Management information systems tend to focus on the two highest levels, since these represent *management* as opposed to *supervisory* or actual operational activities. However, it is not possible to construct an MMIS in isolation from the other levels. Usually a good MMIS seeks to integrate all levels in such a way that data are distilled into successively more aggregated information as it is used for higher-level management activities. For instance, the status of individual orders is an appropriate information output at the level of operational control. At the management control level, summaries of overdue orders by product might be appropriately reported in terms of the percentage of overdue orders and average number of days overdue. At the strategic planning level, concern would be with remedying problems of overdue orders by new resource commitments—hiring new people to fill orders or developing a more efficient order-processing system. At this level, overall cost information is necessary to answer such questions as: How much can we afford to spend to improve order processing? and, What impact will better order processing have on our business?

Thus, strategic planning is concerned with relatively few big questions: What business are we in? What are our objectives? How do we want to go about pursuing our objectives? What overall alignments of resources do we wish to commit to this pursuit? Consequently, strategic planning information is broad and aggregated. For instance, strategic decisions require much more information that is generated outside the organization than do lower level decisions. Information about such environmental entities as competitors and government regulation is very important at this level.

Management control is concerned with making sure committed resources are used in the best way possible to achieve objectives. Thus, management control information is generally more detailed than strategic planning information, and it is more likely to be generated inside the organization. Of course, in this regard the MMIS is less internally oriented than other functional information systems because of its intrinsic link to *customers*.

At the operational control level, emphasis is on the control of individual transactions and projects, with consequently greater informational detail being required. At this level, information is primarily internally generated.

The Structure of the MMIS

Having discussed the conceptual foundations of an MMIS, we next consider the physical system. What does an MMIS look like? What are its constituent parts? Is it something more than the computer? These questions may be answered by describing the primary visible (physically apparent) elements of an MMIS—hardware, software, data base, procedures, and personnel.

Hardware

The hardware element of an MMIS is the most visible part. Hardware for a computer system consists of equipment which prepares data for input to the computer; input devices; the central processing unit (CPU) ("the computer," to most people), which performs computation, stores data, and controls the overall system operation; and output devices. A simple system might look like that of Figure 1-3 which shows a keypunch machine (a device which punches holes in cards to represent data) as the data preparation device; a card reader as the input device; a CPU and a printer as the output device.

Many other pieces of equipment can be used instead of the ones represented in Figure 1-3. Keydisk systems, paper tape punches, and cathode ray tube (CRT) devices may be used for data preparation. Data input may be via remote terminals, paper tape readers, optical scanners and magnetic character readers. Output devices include CRT displays, graph plotters and microfilm devices. Secondary data storage, that which is outside the CPU, is often incorporated into such systems in the form of magnetic tapes and magnetic disks.[16]

The simple diagram of Figure 1-3 does not indicate the complexity of the

---

[16] For detailed discussions of these hardware elements, see H. C. Lucas, Jr., *Computer Based Information Systems in Organizations*, Science Research Associates Inc., 1973.

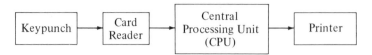

FIGURE 1-3 Typical computer hardware system

hardware configurations in common usage in modern information systems. Figure 1-4 shows the equipment configuration for the information system for the Wood Products Group of the Weyerhaeuser Company when it was in an early stage of development.[17] Although this system goes beyond the scope of marketing information, its primary application at this early stage of development was the processing of order and shipment information, the fundamental transactional data which form the basis for any marketing information system.

In noncomputer information systems, the system hardware consists of typewriters used to prepare and input data to the system, calculators which process it, filing cabinets in which it is stored, and reports generated for management use.

Software

Software is the term used to describe the computer programs which guide the physical operation of the system. Since a computer is really just an electronic device that must be given detailed directions if it is to do anything useful, it requires instructions. Instructions are input to the computer in the same way as data, but software serves to direct the manipulations that the computer performs on data. Some of these instructions are in the form of special programs for performing sets of calculations, such as processing a payroll. Some are *operating programs,* which become a permanent part of the system in that they direct the computer system regarding the performance of its routine functions (e.g., sorting) and the translation of coded programs into machine language, and data management programs which "manage" the organization of and access to the data base.

To understand this distinction between specialized programs, or *applications programs,* and operating programs, consider that you have written a set of instructions which tells the computer to take a number previously punched on a card and add it to another number. You would first need to tell the computer through a set of appropriate symbols in your program to "read" the number from the card. The *operating program* provides the detailed instructions to the computer to permit it to actually accomplish the read operation. Your program,

---

[17] Taken from R. A. Kronenberg, "Weyerhaeuser's Management Information System," *Datamation,* May 1967, p. 30. Reprinted with permission of *Datamation,*® copyright 1967 by Technical Publishing Company, Greenwich, Connecticut, 06830.

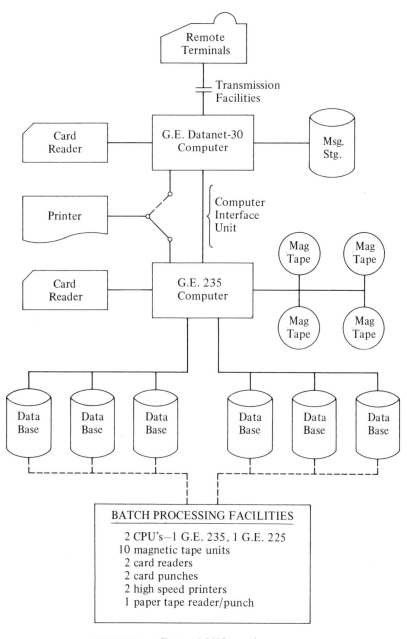

FIGURE 1-4 Typical MIS configuration

which involves read instructions, an add instruction, and many others, is an *applications program;* that is, a specialized program to perform a specific task, such as calculating a quality point average based on inputs of grades in a number of courses.

The software of a noncomputer information system is the set of procedures which tell someone how to perform the operations required to produce the desired system output. A set of instructions as to how to calculate the average order size based on the day's collection of orders would represent an applications program in such a system.

Data base

The system's data base is the collection of data stored on magnetic tape, disk packs, and other physical storage media. Other forms of storage such as cards and documents may form a part of the data base as well.

Data are recorded on *files* in the data base. A typical transaction processing run will take input data and process them in some fashion against one or more files in the data base to produce output. For instance, an invoice amount is input and added to the customer's outstanding balance in the data base to produce a new balance for the customer. This new balance is the desired output, and it may also be stored in the data base in place of, or in addition to, the old balance.

The files associated with noncomputer systems are usually documents; but they may also be other media such as microfilm or microfiche. The file organization may be alphabetic or numerically coded by social security number or some other identifier, just as with the file structure of a computerized system.

In either a computerized or a noncomputerized system, the data base contains both the status and history of the organization's activities as well as data on competitors and other environmental institutions which do or can affect the organization. The hardware and software of the system are more visible than the data base. Thus, when an information system is being developed and designed, much attention is often paid to the selection of hardware and software while relatively less attention is given to data base design. Since the inclusion or exclusion of data items from the data base largely determines whether it will ever be available at reasonable cost to the organization, these data base decisions may be the most critical ones in information systems design.

Procedures

Procedures are the instructions which guide both the user and the operator in the use of an information system. User instructions specify such things as the range of applicability and the limitations of various applications programs and instructions for the preparation of input to the system. Operating instructions direct computer system operators in the actual execution of the various elements of software.

In a noncomputerized system, much the same is true. So-called systems and procedures analysis has been conducted in organizations for many decades. Such analysis produces procedures for recording and updating data, preparing reports, and performing many of the repetitive tasks of the organization, such as answering inquiries concerning a customer's account balance and preparing monthly sales summaries.

For both computerized and manual systems, procedures manuals are usually provided and available to organizational personnel. These provide necessary guidance for the use of the system. Often consultants, such as computer analysts and programmers, are also made available to aid potential users in preparing programs and associated data for input into the system.

Personnel

Information systems, however sophisticated their computers may be, are operated, directed, and managed by people. Indeed, the common layman's perception of an electronic brain operating independently of humans is rendered almost laughable when one considers the number of people required to effectively and efficiently operate even the most sophisticated information systems.

The job titles associated with virtually every information system include computer operator, systems analyst, programmer, keypunch operator, and key-disk operator. Added to these jobs on the operating level of information systems are those management positions directly related to *managing the information system* and the user, management, and analyst's tasks related to *designing the organization's information system.*

The involvement of people in the organization's information system has changed somewhat as computerized information systems have matured. Early in the computer era, emphasis was placed on the *operating* of the system. Skilled computer analysts and programmers were hired to develop applications programs so that the computer could take over activities which had previously been handled manually. After this was accomplished, attention turned to the use of the computer in performing higher-level activities, such as those related to management control and strategic planning.

Unfortunately, despite the fact that the information system has great value in these areas, many business firms found that computer analysts were not necessarily performing these broader activities on a cost-effective basis. Large and costly programming projects were often found to have little impact on the organization. Where this was recognized, attention turned to the *management of management information systems.* Essentially, this emphasis simply involved the application of the same principles of management control which were applied elsewhere in the organization to the control of the MIS. New projects had to be justified based on whether the anticipated benefits to the organization were worth the costs of developing each new application. Often, it was discovered that the desires of computer analysts to do interesting and innovative things outweighed the organization's overall needs and limitations.

Despite the achievement of a degree of management control over the MIS, it was recognized that the introduction of a computer system into the organization had often been accomplished without a realistic assessment of the organization's need for information, its goals, and limitations regarding money, skills, and the level of sophistication of its managers. Sophisticated systems were introduced into organizations managed by people without much sophistication. This led to organizational difficulties; for example, managers might refuse to use the system for the originally intended purpose. Attention has now turned from management control of the MIS to the *planning and design of an MIS which will fit into the organization and serve its needs.* This has led to new emphasis being placed on the job of the systems designer; on the inclusion of more people into the design process (e.g., information system users); and on the creation of new jobs, such as that of the information analyst, a systems oriented person who works with managers to define and specify their information requirements.[18]

Summary

An understanding of the potential roles for a marketing management information system requires an understanding of the full implications of the basic constituent terms *marketing, management, information,* and *system* as well as of some meaningful compound terms such as *information systems.* This chapter reviews and illustrates the important ideas underlying each of these terms and thereby operationally defines an MMIS.

The MMIS can be thought of either as a part of the overall organizational information system or as an independent entity. In either instance, the objective of a true MMIS is to go beyond the level of data processing to a system which produces information that directly supports management decision making. Such a system may support decision making at any of a variety of levels—strategic planning, management control, or operational control—but the most significant MMIS is one which operates at the levels of strategic planning and management control.

At whatever level, the MMIS is made up of hardware, software, a data base, procedures, and personnel. These common elements may be realized in terms of

---

[18] See R. L. Ashenhurst (ed.), "Curriculum Recommendations for Graduate Professional Programs in Information Systems: A Report of the ACM Curriculum Committee on Computer Education for Management," *Communications of the ACM,* vol. 15, no. 5 (May 1972), pp. 363–398.

a computerized system or in terms of a much simpler manual system. In either case, the careful specification of the nature of each of these elements and the precise role to be played by each are among the most critical aspects of designing and developing an MMIS which is to be truly useful and supportive of marketing decision making.

EXERCISES

1. Give your opinion of the following statement: Marketing is concerned with the efficient distribution of products.
2. Explain the following definition: Management is working through others to achieve organizational objectives.
3. Distinguish between data and information.
4. Using the five major structural elements of an MMIS—hardware, software, data base, procedures and personnel—describe why the MMIS is truly a *system*.
5. Does the typical family have an information system? If so, describe it in terms of the five basic structural elements.
6. How is a management information system different from a data processing system? In what ways are they the same?
7. Distinguish between organizational effectiveness and efficiency.
8. What is the *modular* approach to systems design?
9. Describe the benefits and problems associated with an integrated data base.
10. Why wouldn't it be feasible to design separate information systems to support each of the hierarchical levels of the MMIS? In other words, why not have a separate system for transaction processing, operational control information, management control information, and strategic planning information?
11. What is the most important distinction between strategic planning and management control?

REFERENCES

Ackoff, R. L. *A Concept of Corporate Planning.* New York: Wiley, 1970.

Churchman, C. W.; Ackoff, R. L.; and Arnoff, E. L. *Introduction to Operations Research.* New York: Wiley, 1957.

Diebold, J. "Bad Decisions on Computer Use." *Harvard Business Review,* January–February 1969.

Gibson, L. D., et al. "An Evolutionary Approach to Marketing Information Systems." *Journal of Marketing,* April 1973, pp. 2–6.

Hamilton, W. J. and Moses, M. A. "A Computer-Based Corporate Planning System." *Management Science,* October 1974, pp. 148–159.

Hodge, B. "The Computer in Management Information and Control Systems." *Data Management,* December 1974, pp. 26–30.

Lucas, H. C., Jr. "A Descriptive Model of Information Systems in the Context of the Organization." *Data Base,* Winter 1973, pp. 27–39.

McKinsey and Co. "Unlocking the Computer's Profit Potential." *Computers and Automation,* April 1969.

Murdick, R. G. "MIS Development Procedures." *Journal of Systems Management,* December 1970, pp. 22–26.

Nolan, R. L. "Computer Data Base: The Future Is Now." *Harvard Business Review,* Sept.–Oct. 1973, pp. 98–114.

2

Information and Information Systems
for Decision Support

The important role of and need for information and information systems in marketing is not universally understood. Most business firms and other organizations certainly recognize the need for data at the levels of transaction processing and operational control, those levels involving doing the organization's basic work and seeing that it gets done. However, at higher management levels, many organizations have developed information systems that are primarily accounting oriented and inward looking rather than marketing oriented and outward looking.

This chapter emphasizes the need for marketing information, in terms of the uses to which the information is put, and the need in most organizations for a system to provide this information in an efficient and effective fashion.

The Need for Marketing Information

There is, perhaps, more of a general awareness among marketing people than among other people in organizations of the need for current factual information. Marketers are very aware of their need to know about things that are happening in the world outside their organization because that is where the major impact is felt from their activities (selling, advertising, promoting sales, etc.) By contrast, for example, the activities of a production manager have impact mostly within the organization.

Marketing managers are familiar with and use a wide variety of different kinds of data, much of it reflecting phenomena which are difficult to assess and measure. For instance, advertising managers can receive research data on the perceived meaning to potential customers of contemplated advertisements. Such "impression studies" utilize personal interviews to determine what feature was outstanding about a printed ad, what message it conveyed, and how credibly the message was conveyed. Advertising managers also have available to them the results of sample data describing television viewing patterns of American households and individuals by sex and age groups for a number of past weeks to aid in decisions about future media advertising that they may do.

Similar data are available to marketing managers about other aspects of their responsibilities. For instance, impressions data may be obtained for prospective package designs as well as for advertisements, and retail store audits permit the reporting of retail sales, shelf inventories, retail promotions, retail prices, and store reserve inventories for individual products in individual retail stores.[1]

Thus, marketing managers have a wealth of data of various kinds available to them on a routine basis. However, without an effective MMIS, these data may

---

[1] Starch Inra Hooper, Inc., routinely conducts impression studies, and the A. C. Nielsen Company provides such retail index services on a continuing basis.

not be provided to the right person at the right time so that they can be used for appropriate management purposes such as the support of decision making.

The uses of marketing information

The marketing information which is supplied by a MMIS is necessary for the *support of decision making in the organization*. The term *management decision support system* has been used as an alternative to MIS in an effort to delineate this special variety of system from the myriad varieties which do not directly support decision making.

The decisions which the MMIS must support are as diverse as is the field of marketing. In a manufacturing-oriented firm, for instance, these decisions might be broadly categorized as being in the following areas:

Product development

Pricing

Promotion and advertising

Distribution channels

Purchasing

Physical distribution

Credit

The decisions are at a variety of levels of planning and control. For instance, a strategic planning decision in the area of pricing would involve the choice of a *pricing strategy*. Among the alternative strategies that might be considered are:

1. Get as much profit as you can, as soon as you can.
2. Set a price that will discourage the advent of competitors.
3. Recover your development costs within a specified period.
4. Set a price that will yield your "regular" rate of return.
5. Set a price that will win speediest acceptance of the product.
6. Use the product to enhance the sales of the entire line rather than to yield a profit on itself.[2]

Marketing strategies, which incorporate pricing strategies as well as strategies related to the other marketing decision areas, are based on conclusions and forecasts about the current and future status of the marketplace. These conclusions are derived from marketing information. For instance, a food products manufacturer may have developed a marketing strategy on the basis of conclu-

[2] Alfred R. Oxenfeld, *Developing a Product Strategy* (New York: American Management Association, 1959), p. 338.

sions derived from marketing information which depicted (1) customer concern with the convenience, choice, and diversity offered by food products and (2) dramatically rising consumer expenditures on nonfood items relative to food items.[3] A reasonable marketing strategy based on this information would have been one which emphasized food items with high value-added, great convenience, and the continuous offering of new sizes, forms, and varieties of existing food products. This, coupled with the development of new products which would be addressed to capturing the increasing expenditures of consumers on nonfood items, is a strategy which reflects the direct use of the available marketing information.

If new marketing information becomes available that suggests a change in consumer preferences toward nutritional value and economic value (in terms of ounces per dollar) and if trends change so that food begins to take an increasing share of the consumer's dollar, a different strategy becomes necessary. Such a strategy might involve the pruning of the product line to eliminate uneconomical sizes and varieties; highlighting *value* in advertising, promotion, and packaging; and reemphasis on the "core" food business lines.

Thus, *a change in the information which depicts the status and future of the market dictates a change in the marketing strategy which is chosen by the firm.* So too are choices at other levels in the organization guided by the information which is available. In the credit area, for instance, new information about government regulations might result in an overall *policy* to guide all lower-level decisions involving credit. A common policy today is one which does not permit such factors as race, age, and sex to be used in making credit decisions.

At a lower organizational level, there are decisions regarding the granting of credit to specific customers: Should we ship on a credit basis to XYZ Company? There are also *administrative decisions* regarding how a more significant decision will be handled: Should we require XYZ Company to submit a credit application, or should we simply rely on their credit rating?

These varieties of marketing decisions are based on *information* such as credit ratings and data submitted on applications as well as on *inferences* or *predictions* based on that information. For instance, the choice of an antidiscrimination credit policy might be based on the inference or prediction that a discriminatory policy would lead to bad consequences in the form of law suits, government interference, bad publicity, and a negative social impact by the company. A decision about whether or not to grant credit is based on a prediction of whether or not the customer will pay, how promptly, and with what degree of effort being expended in the form of reminders, dunning letters, etc. The decision about whether or not to have a credit application filled out is one that is based on

[3] This discussion is similar to one by B. A. Bridgewater, Jr., D. K. Clifford, Jr., and T. Hardy in "The Competition Game Has Changed," *Business Horizons,* October 1975.

an assessment of the degree of risk that is involved if the decision is made solely on the basis of the credit rating.

Indeed, information is an important element of all decisions, be they marketing management decisions, overall corporate policy decisions, family decisions, or personal choices.

Decision making and decisions

Table 2-1 shows a simple decision problem described in an abstract fashion.[4] The decision problem is a simple one involving a salesman who must decide whether to spend the next day in an urban or a rural area within his territory. He knows that the sales results he can expect to achieve depend on what sort of weather will be encountered, for on a sunny day the farmers will be off in their fields, making it difficult to contact them, but on a rainy day they will be working near the farmhouse, where they can be contacted easily. On the other hand, the city traffic will be so congested on a rainy day as to prevent the salesman from making many calls. The *payoff table* (2-1) describes the situation for the various outcomes.

The payoff table indicates that the salesman expects to make a profit of $20 if he goes to the city and the day turns out to be sunny, $10 if he makes the same choice and it rains, $15 if he goes to the farm and it is sunny, and $25 if he chooses the farm on a day that turns out to be rainy.

Although this choice situation is obviously very simple, even trivial, when compared to the sorts of marketing decisions involving strategic issues, credit policy, etc., it helps to illustrate the need for and importance of information in every kind of decision making and at every level.

If the salesman who has formulated the decision problem of Table 2-1 is rational, he can only resolve it by asking for *more information.* He might, for instance, choose to watch the TV weather report on the previous evening to get some idea of the *likelihood* of rain.

If his best information is that rain is virtually certain, he can choose to go to

TABLE 2-1 Payoff Table

	State of Nature	
	N_1	N_2
Alternatives	(No Rain)	(Rain)
A_1: city	$20	$10
A_2: farm	$15	$25

[4] Adapted from the author's text, *Quantitative Analysis for Marketing Management* (New York: McGraw-Hill, 1967), with permission of the publisher.

the farm and get a profit of $25, as opposed to the $10 he would get if he went to the city on a rainy day. On the other hand, if he is virtually certain that it will not rain, he can go to the city.

Of course, the weatherman himself may not be "virtually certain" of the next day's weather. He may instead forecast the weather in "likelihood" terms, "a 20 percent chance of rain," as many modern forecasters are wont to do.

If this is the case, decision theory says that the salesman should make the decision on the basis of his *expected profit*.[5] The expected profit for an alternative is calculated as a weighted average of the profits that he can make under the alternative for each of the states of nature which can ensue. In this case the states of nature are rain and no rain, and the likelihoods or probabilities which have been put on each by the weather forecaster are 0.2 and 0.8 respectively. These probabilities are the weights which are used in calculating the expected value.

The expected value associated with the choice to go to the city is

$$E(\text{city}) = 0.8(\$20) + 0.2(\$10) = \$18$$

Similarly, the expected profit from the alternative choice to go to the farm is

$$E(\text{farm}) = 0.8(\$15) + 0.2(\$25) = \$17$$

On the basis of maximizing expected or average *profit,* decision theory would tell the salesman to go to the city because it has a higher expected profit ($18 versus $17) than the profit associated with going to the farm. It is as though he were going to make this identical choice a large number of times, say on every day that the profits are exactly those shown in Table 2-1 and the weather is forecast as a 20 percent chance of rain. The $18 *maximum expected profit* means that if he goes to the city on *every such day,* his average profit will be $18 and that this is higher than he will average if he goes to the farm on every such day.

Of course, sometimes he will go to the city on such a day, it will rain, and he will only make $10. But more often (in fact, four times as often), if he goes to the city on such a day, it will not rain and he will make $20. He will therefore average $18 on each day of this kind, and this is more than the $17 he would average if he went to the farm on each of these days.

Information for decision making

In performing these analyses for the simple decision problem of Table 2-1, we have drawn on two general varieties of *information: value information and likelihood information.*

---

[5] For a more comprehensive statement of this theory as it applies to marketing decisions, see William R. King, *Quantitative Analysis for Marketing Management* (New York: McGraw-Hill, 1967).

Value information. Every decision is based on some predicted sets of *consequences* which are expressed in terms of dollars of profit or some other *value measure*. In Table 2-1, the four possible outcomes are valued in profit terms. These dollar quantities represent information which is absolutely essential if a rational choice is to be made in that situation or in any similar situation.

A glance at Table 2-1 without reference to the dollar figures shows why this is so. Any rational person who is asked whether the salesman should go to the city or country would want to know what difference it would make. The only way this can be answered is in terms of *value information:* It makes a difference because he will value going to the city more on a sunny day and he will value going to the farm more on a rainy day. Specifically, the value which he plans on the four outcomes is in terms of the amount of profit which he will make in each case, and he cannot make a rational choice without knowing what those values are.

Likelihood information. Even with the value information of Table 2-1, however, rational decision making is still not possible without the likelihood information which can be obtained from the weather forecaster. A glance at that table will show that all that it tells even the most sophisticated of us is how much better it is for the salesman to go to the city than to the farm on a sunny day and how much better it is for him to do the reverse on a rainy day. *It does not tell us the best thing to do if we are uncertain about what kind of day it is going to be.* Likelihood information in the form of probabilities, when combined with value information, does provide such guidance, however.

Other decision-related information. While likelihood and value information are essential for making a rational choice in *any* decision problem, marketing managers may not necessarily have information in the form shown in Table 2-1. Their information may be more *raw* although still *decision related.*

For instance, marketing managers may not know that the profit will be $20 in the city on a sunny day. What they know, their *facts* or *data base,* tells what has happened previously. They have records that on rainy days in the city and on rainy days in the country various levels of profit have been produced, etc. So *the values expressed in the table are based on more basic information collected over a period of time.*

So too with the likelihood information provided by the weather forecaster. The forecaster does not know that it will be a good day tomorrow. Neither does he know that the probability of rain is 20 percent. What he does know is that under various sets of conditions, it has rained and not rained with certain frequencies. Thus, his likelihood assessment in the form of a probability of 0.20 is also based on some more basic information.

Models in decision making

The relative roles played by more basic information, value information, and likelihood information lead naturally to the idea of a *model*.

A model is *an abstract representation or relationship which is used to predict*.

Predictive models for likelihoods. Weather forecasters use models, abstract relationships, to predict the likelihood of rain. The model is based on the way in which various factors such as temperature, humidity, cloud formations, and dew points interact to produce rainfall and also on the relative frequency with which various combinations of these factors have, in fact, produced rain in the past.

For instance, the model might be an equation such as [6]

Probability of rainfall $= 0.286$(temp.) $+ 0.3$(dew point) $+ 0.91$(humidity) $+ \ldots$

This equation expresses in numerical terms a relationship between some factors such as temperature and the probability of rain. The numerical quantities in the equation are estimated by statistical means, using a technique called multiple regression analysis,[7] from historical data which describe how often it has rained when various combinations of the factors were present.

The model can be used for predictive purposes by simply inserting data on the factors (temperature, dew point, etc.) and performing the calculations of multiplying 0.286 times the temperature, adding that to 0.3 multiplied by the dew point, etc. The result is, according to the model, the predicted likelihood of rain.

Predictive models for values. The dollar values reflected in Table 2-1 must also be developed using predictive models. This may be done in a sophisticated way using a regression model or in a simpler way using a cross-classification model. For example, the manager can list all the occasions in the past for which he has records and identify, for each day, which of the four sets of circumstances in Table 2-1 is represented by each day. Sometimes the salesman has gone to the city and it has rained, so those days would be classified in the city-rain category. Other days, he has gone to the city and it has not rained, so those would be classified into the city-no-rain category.

Such a categorization, along with a list of the profit outcomes for each day, provides a basis for a cross-classification model. The manager might, for example, simply calculate the average profit which has actually resulted from each

[6] Models used for these purposes are somewhat more complex than that shown. See R. G. Miller, "The Probability of Rain," in T. M. Tanur et al., *Statistics: A Guide to the Unknown* (San Francisco: Holden-Day, 1972).

[7] See any basic statistics text or H. J. Claycamp, "Correlation and Regression Methods," in R. Ferber (ed.), *Handbook of Marketing Research* (New York: McGraw-Hill, 1974), sec. II, pt. E, chap. 5.

of the four kinds of circumstances. The cross-classification plus his average calculation would be his predictive model if he then simply inserts these averages in Table 2-1 as estimates of the *future values* to be anticipated under each circumstance.

Alternatively, he might wish to adjust the model to account for *inflation*. To do this, he might first inflate each past profit figure to better reflect the current level of the economy and then average these adjusted figures to get a prediction of the profit which can be anticipated in each circumstance now or in the future.

In any case, the translation of the basic data into useful value information requires the use of a model, a relationship which is used for predictive purposes.

Mental models. Of course, many choices are made without reference to regression equations or even averages of past history. How then can one say that a model is necessary?

The answer to this question lies in the idea of a mental model, an abstract relationship which exists in the mind of a decision maker. Indeed, each of us uses models in making every decision in our lives, whether it is the choice of a new car, a new husband or wife, or a new product. We do this simply because we cannot think in terms of the complexities of the real world. Rather, we think in terms of abstractions that sum up its salient features and relationships. These mental models permit us to make predictions and evaluations, much as the management scientist does with his formal models. However, for many important decisions, the process unfolds in the inner recesses of the human mind.

For instance, in selecting an automobile for purchase, one does not evaluate all aspects of each prospective car. Rational decision makers choose those attributes of the auto that are most important to them and neglect many relatively unimportant attributes. The purchaser then mentally weighs each available car in terms of these important attributes. A buyer who does this in an unsophisticated way may simply have a mental checklist for evaluating the car, for example:

Does it have good fuel economy?

Does it have a sporty image?

Will it comfortably accommodate five people?

Can I afford it?

Buyers who are more sophisticated will consider *trade-offs* in their mental models, for example:

How much more can I afford to pay to get an additional mile per gallon in fuel economy?

Would I be willing to give up the capacity for one passenger in order to save $500?

At whatever level of sophistication such thinking is done, a *mental model* is being used because the real-world problem is treated in abstract terms which deal only with the most important factors and their relationships. This is the very essence of a *model*. Even if the model is not an explicit one, it is still related to value, likelihood, and other basic information, as illustrated above.

Time-sensitive and knowledge-sensitive decisions

Most of the foregoing discussion assumes that the decision maker is making a knowledge-sensitive decision—one in which the value or worth of the eventual outcome is based more on the *quality* of the choice that is made than it is on the *timeliness* of that choice. Time-sensitive choices are those where the outcome depends more on doing something than on the quality of the choice. For instance, an individual who is standing in the middle of a busy street with an automobile bearing down on him or her is in a situation that requires a time-sensitive choice; it is more important to do something (get out of the way) than it is to carefully consider what to do (whether to run toward the left or the right curb).

Although a common image of a decisive leader is that derived from situations requiring time-sensitive decisions (such as those on the battlefield in wartime), most important marketing decisions are more knowledge-sensitive than time-sensitive. That is, *the quality of the choice* is the most important determinant of the outcome, not the timeliness with which it is made.

It should be pointed out, however, that timeliness may itself be one of the important aspects of the quality of the choice that is made. For instance, deciding whether to enter a new market depends importantly on *when* a company chooses to do so. If one is restricted, because of timing considerations, to following other companies into the market, the timing element may doom the strategy to failure. In such a case the earlier entrant takes advantage of large initial sales to achieve lower production costs and lower prices, thereby making it difficult for a follower to compete in the market.

For knowledge-sensitive choices, it is important and proper to consider (1) the models that are used in the decision process, even if they are only mental models, and (2) the information which is necessary if a good choice is to be made. The variety of choice situations requires both analysis and the collection of detailed information. Indeed, when decisions are being made on a continuing basis, they warrant the development of a *system* to support the decision process.

The Need for an Information System

Since marketing management information must be collected in a fashion which permits it to be used in a variety of decision situations by various individuals, a *system* is needed for collecting, analyzing, and disseminating information.

The information explosion that we hear so much about demands that systems be developed for coping with the ever-greater production of data. As Estes has said:

. . . management information is growing by the microsecond and even nanosecond. We cannot turn off the flow. We had therefore better learn to control it—and we are already running late.[8]

Simply controlling the flow of data has become such a difficult problem that it requires systematization. This need is particularly acute in marketing, where the large *variety* of data compounds the problem of the quantity of data. The marketing manager is routinely called upon to deal with data such as the following:

Audit and panel data

Questionnaire replies

Attitudinal data on consumers

Motivational information

Psychological trait data on customers

Product image data

Media viewing patterns

The magnitude and diversity of such data are so great as to preclude unsystematic processing and use.

The way in which the domain of marketing reaches out into the environment also requires complex systems. One firm, for example, established the following objectives for an *information system* which was to be used by marketing managers.

Assure the availability, on a timely basis, of credible and comprehensive information about the capabilities, and the options for their employment, of key competitors.

Determine the manner in which the actions of key competitors might affect current organizational interests.

Continuously monitor and provide credible and comprehensive information on situations and contingencies in the competitive and environmental systems in the marketplace which might have an impact on the interests of the organization.

Maintain comprehensive and reliable information on political, economic, legal, social, and technological systems affecting the posture of the organization.

[8] H. M. Estes, "Will Managers Be Overwhelmed by the Information Explosion?" *Armed Forces Management,* December 1966, p. 84.

Achieve efficiency and eliminate unnecessary duplication of effort for the collection, analysis, and dissemination of intelligence for the organization.[9]

Although these objectives represent a fairly sophisticated level of marketing information requirements, they well illustrate the level of complexity which may be involved in developing information to support marketing decision making. In effect, such information represents basic data on which predictions of value and likelihood information must be based. Such predictions are made using models of some variety.

To even attempt to address the broad diversity of sources and uses for such data without systematization would be utter folly. No individual or group could reasonably be expected to be aware and, much less, to have evaluated such a wide range of data. Therefore, any action taken without such a system is necessarily made without the full information which could contribute to that action.

Even subjective personally derived information needs to be systematized. The competitor's "slip of the lip" will stand a much greater chance of being caught and passed on to the key decision makers if the individual who hears it is aware of a need and of a system where it can be evaluated, put into its proper context, and highlighted as potentially useful intelligence.

To systematize the gathering, analysis, and dissemination of business information questions such as the following need to be answered:

What needs to be known?

Where can the data be obtained?

Who will gather the data?

How will the data be gathered?

Who will analyze and interpret the data?

How will extracted information be stored most efficiently for equally efficient future retrieval?

How can extracted information be disseminated to the proper parties at the right time for consideration?

How will the system be protected from "leakage" and sabotage?

When the necessary choices are made and implemented, based on questions such as those above, an information system has been created. Unless the marketing decision which the information is to support is a simple unique one which can be approached on a somewhat ad hoc basis, reasonable answers to such questions may dictate that a computer system be utilized for effective storage and retrieval operations. In any case, some variety of system, composed of personnel, hard-

[9] Adapted from David I. Cleland and William R. King, "Competitive Business Intelligence Systems," *Business Horizons,* December 1975.

ware, software, procedures, policies, and activities for resolving the above questions, is essential if any sense is to be made from the wide range of basic information which is available.

The Value of Information

The need for information to support marketing decision making cannot be justified solely on the grounds thus far used. This is so because almost any data could be evaluated to be *potentially useful* to some marketing decision maker, in some situation, at some time. On these grounds, a system might be justified as a means for collecting, processing, and disseminating almost any variety of information.

What is needed is a basis for analyzing whether the information is sufficiently valuable to warrant the cost of incorporating it into a system (cost/value analysis). The cost portion of the cost/value relationship is rather well defined. It is relatively easy to estimate how much it will cost to collect, process, and disseminate an item of information. The value part of the assessment is less clear because *it involves attributes of the information itself* (rather than attributes of a process for doing something to the information, i.e., collecting, processing, disseminating, as with cost estimates).

The value or worth of information is the value placed on it by the decision maker.[10] Although some people in some situations might suggest that all data have value (the belief that knowledge is power), it seems clear that only information, or evaluated data, has any value to most of us. A table of random numbers can have value, but only to someone who knows how to apply it to problem solving; to most people, it is a worthless collection of symbols. Thus a simple proposition that information has value because, by definition, it has been evaluated, and data do not since they are unevaluated would seem to fulfill the need for a concept of the value of information.

There are, however, vast gradations of worth within the category of valued data, or information. Some information can be intuitively determined to have great *potential value,* such as information concerning the next card to be dealt in a hand of blackjack, and some little value to most people, the number of grains of sand on a beach, for example. The intuitive value of information has to do with the *use to which it may be put in guiding decision making.* Information about the next card to be dealt can influence our bet and hence our winnings in a game of cards, but few of us have any opportunity to make use of data concerning the number of grains of sand on a beach.

---

[10] Note the distinction between the previously discussed idea of *value information,* which describes the values that a decision maker places on the possible *outcomes* of a decision problem, and the *value of information,* the *worth* attributed to information, as introduced here.

Of course, it can be argued that the card information is really information (evaluated data) and that the sand-grain information is really just raw data. However, consider how that distinction is made, that is, by *the conceptual process of evaluating data and thus converting it into information.*

A basic value-of-information concept

A basic concept of the value of information has to do with the *influence of the information on the choice process.*

Suppose the decision problem is that shown in Table 2-2 and that, on the basis of the best available information concerning values and likelihoods, the decision maker has chosen A_1 over A_2. This choice has been made on the basis of the expected value calculations which show A_1 to have an expected value of $60 while A_2 has an expected value of only $56, that is:

$$0.5 \ (\$80) + 0.5 \ (\$40) = \$60$$
$$0.5 \ (\$82) + 0.5 \ (\$30) = \$56$$

Now, suppose that new information on likelihoods becomes available. Indeed, suppose that the new probability of the first state of nature is known to be 0.7 rather than 0.5. The revised expected value calculations would then be

$$0.7 \ (\$80) + 0.3 \ (\$40) = \$68$$
$$0.7 \ (\$82) + 0.3 \ (\$30) = \$63.40$$

According to this new information, the choice should still be A_1 since it still has a higher expected value.

What value does the new likelihood information (that the probability is 0.7 rather than 0.5) have to the decision maker? Since it did not lead him to change his choice of A_1, does it have any value at all?

According to one basic view of the value of information, it does not. That is, *information which does not influence action does not have value; information which influences action does have value.* Thus, according to this value-of-information concept, the information that the probability is 0.7 rather than 0.5 had no value, since it did not lead to a change in the action taken, or choice made, by the decision maker.

TABLE 2-2 Formal Description of a Decision Problem

Actions	States of Nature	
	0.5	0.5
A_1	$80	$40
A_2	$82	$30

On the other hand, a message that said that the probability of the first state of nature was 0.9 would have value according to this criterion since it would lead to a change in the choice from A_1 to A_2. Indeed, a little algebra shows that for any probability (for the first state of nature) which is less than $10/12$, A_1 is the best action to choose, and for any probability above $10/12$, A_2 is best. For a probability of exactly $10/12$, the two actions are equally attractive.

Thus, any message which changed the decision maker's assessment of the probability of the first state of nature from 0.5 to any number in the interval from zero to $10/12$ would have no value, but any change which gave a new probability greater than $10/12$ would have value.

Of course, this basic concept of the value of information is overly simplistic, since it does not account for a variety of attributes that most people would value in information. For instance, what if the revised probability were 0.0001? In such a case one could intuitively be virtually certain (unless there were great possibility for error in the estimation of the probabilities) that the first state of nature would occur and, hence, that A_1 was the best action to select. This would give most people a great feeling of certainty and security in their choice of A_1, and *most of us would place value on this* even though the new information had not changed our choice but had merely given us greater confidence that we had made the right choice.

On the other hand, a message that the probability is 0.83 would also have value to many people since, while it would still lead to a choice of A_1, it would tell us that only a small mistake in the probability assessment could lead to a wrong choice (because $10/12 = 0.834$). Most people would want to gather more information before making an important decision in such a situation; or at least they would feel uncomfortable about their selection of A_1 and would stand ready to alter their choice quickly if it did turn out to be wrong. In either case, the information has value which is not reflected by the simple concept of whether or not it leads to a change in the actions taken by the decision maker.

Criteria for evaluating information

The literature and practice of accounting has provided standards by which to measure the value of information which may prove to be most useful in the design and use of an MMIS. The American Accounting Association's definitive statement [11] recommends four basic criteria for evaluating potential accounting information. [12]

---

[11] American Accounting Association, *A Statement of Basic Accounting Theory*, 1965.

[12] A similar approach has been taken in the marketing context by B. Wilkinson, "A Systems Approach to Marketing Information," *Journal of Systems Management*, October 1969, pp. 7–10; but the accounting approach is adopted here because of its greater utility.

Relevance

Verifiability

Freedom from bias

Quantifiability

Relevance, the primary criterion, refers to the usefulness of the information for the actions of the data recipient. *Verifiability* means essentially reliability, which suggests that repeated measures or observations would yield identical conclusions. *Freedom from bias* and *quantifiability* are self-explanatory.

In addition to these four criteria, the AAA also has suggested five guidelines for the communication of information: appropriateness to expected use, disclosure of significant relationships, inclusion of environmental data, uniformity of practice within and among entities, and consistency of practices over time. While these guidelines are oriented toward accounting, they have some relevance for other types of communications. It should be noted that there is some overlap between the four criteria and the five guidelines.

Snavely expanded upon the AAA categorization and has also clarified the relationships among the criteria.[13] His criteria, as shown in Figure 2-1, are four levels of qualities that contribute to the value of information. At the first and primary level, the sole, all-important criterion is *usefulness.* Subsidiary to this, at the second level, are the criteria of relevance, reliability, understandability, significance, sufficiency, and practicality.

According to Snavely (as shown in Figure 2-1), there are three types of relevant information: that which assists in the evaluation of management, management policies, and the value of the firm. These are the third-level criteria that are subsidiary to relevance. Reliability gives rise to the third-level qualities of freedom from bias and verifiability, which are interpreted as the components of reliability. Likewise, the elements of understandability are quantifiability, consistency with user concepts, comparability, and simplicity. Decision orientation is the subsidiary criterion of significance; and timeliness and benefits in excess of costs are the components of practicality.

As with the AAA criteria, Snavely's criteria are oriented toward the evaluation of potential accounting information; but many of the criteria, especially at the higher levels in Snavely's proposal, are applicable to a broad spectrum of information types.

In a sense, what these various criteria do is to operationally define, however qualitatively, what is meant by the *usefulness* and, hence, the *value* of information. In developing criteria which make explicit the various subtleties and shadings of meanings inherent in most people's concept of information, the criteria of Figure 2-1 can be useful guides to information evaluation:

[13] H. J. Snavely, "Accounting Information Criteria," *Accounting Review,* April 1967.

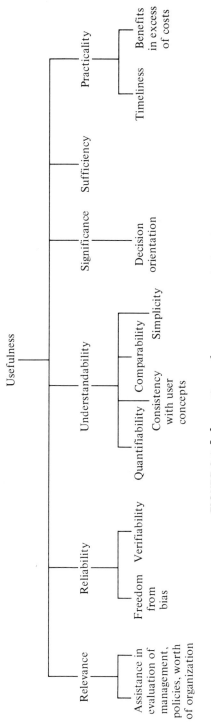

FIGURE 2-1 Information value assessment structure

1. Information which is useful has value.
2. Useful information is that which is relevant, reliable, understandable, significant, sufficient, and practical.
3. Information is relevant insofar as it aids in the evaluation of management, policies, or the worth of the organization.
4. Reliable information is verifiable and free *from bias*.
5. Understandable information has quantifiability, comparability, and simplicity and is consistent with user concepts (e.g., it is expressed in terms that the user understands).
6. Significant information is decision oriented.
7. Sufficient information is adequate to support a choice.
8. Practical information is timely and yields benefits in excess of costs.

These guides may be used both to better understand the meaning of the value of information and as a checklist in assessing information value. Of course, individual items of information possess each of these attributes to varying degrees. These statements should be interpreted to mean that more is better, for example, the more verifiable information is, and the greater freedom it has from bias, the more reliable it is. Obviously, the criteria cannot be applied in a "necessary and sufficient" sense. Rather, the criteria can be used as guides to thinking about the worth of information and as guides to the design of information systems.

Consider a systems designer's decision about whether a specific item of information should be provided by the MMIS to the marketing manager. Suppose, for example, that it is proposed that the standard industrial classification (SIC) code number for each customer be added to each invoice.[14] To assess the value of this proposed new information, we might ask the questions noted on the left of Table 2-3, which involve each of the criteria from Figure 2-1.

Table 2-3 shows that the proposed information can be justified on each of the six primary criteria in terms of nearly every one of the lower-level explications of each criterion. Thus, it is assessed to be valuable. If it had not met each of these major criteria, it would be assessed to be less valuable; perhaps sufficiently less valuable so as to not warrant being collected and used.

A concept of information value such as that given in Figure 2-1 provides a conceptual framework for understanding and thinking about information value in practical terms. Moreover, the concept is an operational guide to decisions which must be made during the process of MMIS design and development because some of the most crucial design issues are those involving the choice of which items of information to include into the MMIS data base and which to leave out.

These choices inherently involve information value since any choice concerning the inclusion of an item of information into an MMIS may be stated in

[14] The SIC code is a government designation which describes the industry categories represented by a firm's activities and products.

TABLE 2-3 Assessing the Value of Information

Is it *relevant?*	Yes, it can aid in the evaluation of *policies* related to allocation of sales effort to various customer groups.
Is it *reliable?*	Yes, the government assigns the code on an objective basis and its accuracy is readily verifiable.
Is it *understandable?*	Yes, it is quantifiable, simple, comparable to other code designations which are used, and understood by users based on past uses for other purposes.
Is it *significant?*	Yes, it can aid in making specific identifiable decisions.
Is it *sufficient?*	Yes, if a four-digit code is used, it is adequate to distinguish among appropriate customer groups.
Is it *practical?*	Yes, we can obtain it in a timely fashion and at very low cost. The cost of placing it on each invoice is very small.

cost/value terms; for example, Is this information sufficiently valuable to warrant incurring the costs of collecting, processing, and disseminating it? If the answer is positive, the information should be included into the MMIS data base; otherwise, it should not be included.

Summary

Marketing information is necessary if good marketing choices are to be made since the range of consequences which can emanate from a decision is normally quite wide. Good decision making may therefore be thought of as a process for selecting the high quality consequences from the wide range of possible consequences in any choice situation. Such a selection process is necessarily based on *information*.

Information about the *value* of various consequences and the *likelihood* of various consequences may be combined in order to arrive at a rational choice in any decision situation. This is accomplished in terms of a *decision model,* which may be a rather simple depiction of the decision situation, such as a payoff array.

Other *predictive models* may be used to convert raw data into predictions of future values or likelihoods. These models may be either formal or informal. Informal mental models are used by everyone in making subjective choices, since everyone thinks in terms of an abstract mental representation of a real-world decision situation. More formal models are useful in knowledge-sensitive decision situations—those in which the outcome is primarily a function of the quality of the alternative which is chosen.

Since the information and models which are the essence of informed choice are so diverse, some variety of information system is usually necessary in order that the information be collected, processed, and disseminated efficiently and effectively.

However, some objective criterion of value for information must be developed if the MMIS is to be developed on a cost/value basis. This is so because virtually any item of data could be justified to be potentially useful in some vague way. Although there is no single such criterion, there is a basic principle on which information value may be based, namely, that *management information* should be valued in terms of its influence on the decision process.

This principle has been translated into operational terms through a set of criteria which at the broadest level translate information usefulness into the subcriteria of relevance, reliability, understandability, significance, sufficiency, and practicality. Some of these subcriteria may be further subdivided to form a checklist for the evaluation of information. Such a checklist provides basic insight into the cost/value relationships basic to decisions concerning the inclusion or exclusion of information into the MMIS.

EXERCISES

1. Describe *marketing strategies* which might apply to each of the following decision areas: product development, pricing, promotion, advertising, distribution channels, purchasing, physical distribution, and credit.

2. For any one strategy in each of the decision areas in question 1, delineate a series of management and administrative decisions which might be required of the managers who must implement and operationalize the strategy.

3. Make a list of information requirements for each of the decisions in question 2. Identify those decisions that require drawing inferences from predictions.

4. What choice would you make in the decision situation of Table 2-1 if you had no information other than that given there, that is, no likelihood information? What is the basis for your choice? Do you think it is a very good basis for decision making?

5. When decisions are made on the basis of maximum expected profit or minimum expected loss, there is always the possibility of achieving an outcome, in any single decision situation, which is less than the expectation. Explain why this is so.

6. If a decision situation is to be faced only once, making a choice on the basis of an expectation, or average over many repetitions of the situation, might seem to be foolish. Is it? Why or why not?

7. Distinguish between value information and likelihood information in the context of the information requirements you delineated in question 3.

8. Consider how the various predictions or inferences you identified in question 3 could be made using formal models such as those described for values and likelihoods in the chapter.

9. What sort of mental model might you use in a decision about which new auto to purchase? Try to make it explicit by writing down the factors you consider, their relationships to one another, and your overall choice criterion.

10. What basic criteria can be applied in deciding whether to develop a system or whether to let information collection and processing go on rather unsystematically?

11. Describe what is meant by the value of information. How might the concept apply to the kinds of information that are provided to you by the following:
    a. Auto manufacturers in their brochures?
    b. The packages of small appliances?
    c. Television commercials?
    d. Contents lists on food packages?

12. Show, using algebra, that for any probability for the first state of nature which is less than $^{10}/_{12}$ in table 2-2, A_1 is the best action to choose.

13. Evaluate the following in terms of the value of information criteria used in Table 2-3:
    a. A credit rating to be obtained from a credit bureau, in order to decide whether an individual is to be given credit
    b. Information on the sales history of various salespeople, in order to determine who should be given the job of sales manager
    c. Subscriptions to, and analyses of, technical journals in which competitors' researchers are known to publish, in order to ascertain which new products they will introduce
    d. An information system to provide summaries of government regulations which may affect the safety requirements for your products

14. Suppose an evaluation such as that in Table 2-3 turned out to have some positive and some negative responses. How would you evaluate the information?

REFERENCES

American Accounting Association. *A Statement of Basic Accounting Theory,* 1965.

Bass, Frank, et al. (eds.). *Applications of the Sciences in Marketing Management.* New York: Wiley, 1968.

Beaver, W. H. "The Information Content of Annual Earnings and Announcements." *Empirical Research in Accounting, 1968.* Supplement of *Journal of Accounting Research.*

Berenson, Conrad. "Marketing Information Systems." *Journal of Marketing,* October 1969.

Feltham, G. A., and Demski, J. S. "The Use of Models in Information Evaluation." *Accounting Review,* October 1970.

Hayes, R. H. and Nolan, R. L. "What Kind of Corporate Modeling Functions Best?" *Harvard Business Review,* May–June 1974, pp. 102–112.

King, William R. *Quantitative Analysis for Marketing Management.* New York: McGraw-Hill, 1967.

———— and Epstein, Barry J. "Assessing the Value of Information." *Management Datamatics,* September 1976.

Kotler, Philip. *Marketing Management: Analysis, Planning, and Control,* 3d ed. Englewood Cliffs, N.J.: Prentice-Hall, 1976.

Lieberman, A. Z. and Whinston, A. B. "A Structuring of an Events-Accounting Information System." *The Accounting Review,* April 1975, pp. 246–258.

Lucas, H. C., Jr. "Performance and Use of an Information System." *Management Science,* April 1975, pp. 908–919.

Mock, T. J. "Concepts of Information Value and Accounting." *Accounting Review,* October 1971.

3

Information and Decision Models

This chapter demonstrates, using a more sophisticated method than in the previous chapter, the various uses of information in making marketing decisions. The usefulness of information in decision making does not need to be extensively demonstrated. However, the various kinds and levels of information that can be used in a decision situation, the manager's ability to choose among sets of information (just as he chooses among alternatives in a decision problem), and the intrinsic interrelationship between the manager's decision model and the information that he requires are all points that do require demonstration.

Example of a Marketing Decision

The various levels and varieties of information and the various characteristics of that information can best be demonstrated through the use of a specific situation involving a marketing decision. The situation is one involving the choice of whether or not to expand the sales of a recently introduced product which has been sold in a limited number of markets for a limited time. Let us assume that a new consumer product was introduced in a number of market areas near the company's main production facility and now the company faces the decision about whether or not to expand sales beyond that region.

Market potential

A direct approach to the question of marketing expansion in this case is to estimate *market potentials* for new markets in which the product might be sold and make a decision on the basis of those potentials. A market potential is "the total amount of a product . . . which would be sold to a market in a specified time period and under a given set of conditions." [1] Sales potential is the proportion of the market potential that a single firm or brand expects to obtain.

A common approach to the establishment potentials is shown in Table 3-1.[2] The underlying assumption of that table is that consumer families can consume only what their income permits, at least in the long run. Also, that table implicitly reflects the good deal of available empirical evidence that families of similar size, composition, and income levels tend to distribute their consumption expenditures similarly among major categories such as food, clothing, shelter.

Table 3-1 shows the families in a particular county or market area categorized by income level. The number of families in each income group are tabulated along with the average annual expenditure of families in each group on

---

[1] King, William R., "Estimating Market Potential," in R. Ferber (ed.), *Marketing Research Handbook* (New York: McGraw-Hill, 1975) sec. IV, pt. A, chap. 1.

[2] Ibid. Reprinted with permission of publisher.

TABLE 3-1 Market Potential in County A

After-tax Income	Number of Families	Average Annual Expenditure on Product Category Per Family	Total Annual Expenditure on Product Category
Under $1,000	47	$ 14	$ 658
$ 1,000–1,999	167	5	835
2,000–2,999	238	10	2,380
3,000–3,999	466	20	9,320
4,000–4,999	2,427	26	63,102
5,000–5,999	5,900	39	230,100
6,000–7,499	1,263	59	74,517
7,500–9,999	1,004	83	83,332
10,000–14,999	228	183	41,724
15,000 and over	64	395	25,280
Total county potential for product category . . .			$531,248

the product category in question. Such data as those appearing in the middle two columns of Table 3-1 are available from a variety of sources.[3]

The simple calculations shown in Table 3-1 result in an overall market potential assessment of $531,248 for the county in question. Such a potential can then be converted into a sales potential by applying it to the market share which can reasonably be expected for the brand in question. Alternately, the break-even sales level can be compared to it, and the market share required in order to break even can be calculated and assessed as to whether it can reasonably be attained.

Simple cross-classification analysis

The market potential approach is widely used in such circumstances, but it clearly ignores information which is available on how the product has been performing in the areas in which it has been sold. Most people would agree that an approach which takes this information into account would be a better one, but it is not immediately clear how this may be done.

One possible approach is to try to relate sales performance to characteristics of the various market areas. This assumes, of course, that sales performance has been somewhat variable in the various areas. If some relationship can be developed, it may be used as a basis for predicting the sales to be expected in new areas, should expansion of product sales be undertaken.

---

[3] For instance, *Sales and Marketing Management*'s annual issue of "Survey of Buying Power"; the U.S. Department of Commerce's *Survey of Current Business;* Rand McNally's *Commercial Atlas and Marketing Guide;* and the U.S. Census Bureau's *County and City Data Book.*

TABLE 3-2 Cross-Classification of 37 Areas

Average Monthly Sales (Thousands)	Average Income Level							
	5–5.99	6–6.99	7–7.99	8–8.99	9–9.99	10–10.99	11 and over	Total
0–4	0	0	1	0	0	0	0	1
4–8	0	0	1	0	1	0	0	2
8–12	2	0	2	0	0	0	0	4
12–16	1	2	1	0	1	0	0	5
16–20	0	1	2	0	0	1	0	4
20–24	1	1	0	3	1	2	1	9
24–28	0	0	0	1	2	0	1	4
28–32	0	1	0	0	2	1	0	4
Over 32	0	0	1	0	0	3	0	4
Total	4	5	8	4	7	7	2	37

Table 3-2 shows a cross-classification in terms of sales and income levels for the areas in which the product has been sold. Inspection of the table reveals a general tendency for sales to be positively related to income levels; that is, for higher sales to result in areas where income levels are highest.

This conclusion suggests that a strategy of choosing higher-income areas for expansion of product sales might be a reasonable one, although it does not readily provide a basis for predicting the sales level that might be expected.

Regression analysis

If the data of Table 3-2 were expressed in numerical form and plotted on a graph, they might appear as in Figure 3-1. That figure shows a scatter diagram which exhibits a positive correlation between income and sales. Each point of Figure 3-1 represents *one* area in which the product has been sold, that area being described in terms of its average income level and the level of sales which has been experienced.

The line drawn through the scatter of Figure 3-1 is a *regression line,* a straight line which provides the best *fit* to the data and which can be used as a basis for prediction.[4] To use a regression line for predicting the sales to be expected in an area which is under consideration for the product, one need know the average family income in the area. The regression line provides the prediction of sales. (In Figure 3-1, suppose that I_o is the average annual family income

---

[4] See any basic statistics text such as J. Neter, W. Wasserman, and G. A. Whitmore, *Fundamental Statistics for Business and Economics,* 4th ed., (Boston: Allyn & Bacon, 1973).

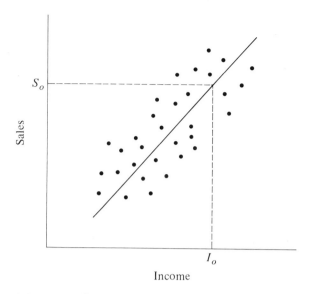

FIGURE 3-1 Correlation between income and sales

in an area which is under consideration. The dotted line shows that S_o would be the expected sales in that area.)

Multiple predictive criteria

If any one measure, such as income, were believed to be an inadequate basis for predicting sales in new market areas, multiple criteria might be used. For instance, Table 3-3 shows one simple approach to analyzing an expansion decision. The purpose of such a table is to determine in a simple fashion, if possible, those factors which contributed to sales success. The sales areas which performed best are listed along with factors believed to be indicative of success. Such factors might be high product-line consumption, high income, youthful population, etc.

Characteristics possessed by the top selling areas are indicated with a check-mark in Table 3-3. For instance, Albuquerque is assessed to have a high income level and youthful population, but not a high consumption level for the product in question.

If a pattern can be established among the various factors considered in Table 3-3, it may provide a basis for the choice of future market areas, although not a basis for the development of quantitative sales predictions. For instance, it might be discovered that high consumption levels by a youthful population are the key

TABLE 3-3 Characteristics of Top Selling Areas

	High Income	Youthful Population	High Product Consumption
Albuquerque	√	√	
Boston	√		
Buffalo			√
Chicago			√
Cleveland			√
Denver	√	√	

factors in determining success. If this is so, it suggests the way in which future markets should be selected.

Multiple regression

The multiple factor approach may be combined with regression analysis. The resulting *multiple regression* approach involves the estimation of a predictive equation of the form

$$y = a_1x_1 + a_2x_2 + a_3x_3 + \ . \ . \ . \ + a_nx_n + b$$

where y is sales and the x's are quantitative variables describing characteristics of the areas (income, population, etc.). The a's and b in the expression are parameters of the regression equation which are estimated from the data for areas in which the product is already sold. This is equivalent to fitting an equation to the data as described in Figure 3-1, although here we are dealing with many predictive variables rather than just one.[5]

A multiple regression equation may be estimated from data in the areas where sales have been conducted. This equation may then be used as a basis for predicting the sales to be expected in other areas. This predictive use requires that data on the predictor variables (the x's) be available for the areas which are being considered. With a knowledge of the x's for the area being considered and a "knowledge" of the a's and b from the application of the regression technique to the historical data, y (sales) may be predicted.

Discriminant analysis

Another approach to the problem which combines features of those previously discussed is that which makes use of discriminant analysis. Suppose that it were possible to classify areas in which the product has been sold as being either good

[5] Ibid.

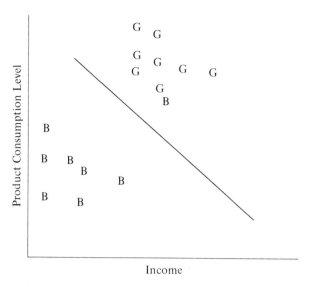

FIGURE 3-2 **Characteristics for good and bad market areas**

or bad performers. When these classifications are described in terms of area characteristics, a diagram such as that of Figure 3-2 might result. This figure locates areas in terms of their income and consumption levels, using G for good and B for bad, depending on how the areas sales performance for our product has been assessed.

Figure 3-2 shows a general pattern of high income and high consumption being associated with good assessments and low income and low consumption being associated with bad assessments. The line drawn between the primarily G and primarily B areas is a *discriminant line,* which can be estimated from historical data in much the same fashion as a regression line.[6]

The estimation of the discriminant line permits areas under consideration for sale of the product to be predicted as being "like" past areas which have been evaluated either as good or bad. This prediction is made on the basis of known predictor values (for income and product consumption) and on the location in the diagram of a proposed area relative to the discriminant line. Proposed areas which are located to the top-right of the line would be predicted to be like past G areas and those located at the lower left would be predicted to be like past B areas.

[6] For a discussion of an application of this, see William R. King, "Marketing Expansion: A Statistical Analysis," *Management Science,* July 1963. For a discussion of the discriminant technique, see D. G. Morrison, "Discriminant Analysis," in R. Ferber (ed.), *Marketing Research Handbook* (New York: McGraw-Hill, 1975), sec. II, pt. E, chap. 8.

Information Analysis of the Marketing Decision Illustration

The purpose of enumerating a number of approaches to one marketing decision problem is to demonstrate the following:

1. The variety of different sensible approaches to the single decision problem
2. The relationship between the approach taken to the problem and the information that is required, or most useful, in solving the problem
3. The various sets of information which are generated by the various solution approaches
4. The relationship between the three factors above and the *value* of each element of information

The reader should note that while the six approaches are quite different, each is a sensible way of thinking about and analyzing the problem of marketing expansion. No one of these approaches can be dismissed out of hand, and the reasonable manager or marketing researcher should consider each of them as a possible way of approaching such a problem.

However, each of the approaches has inherent in it a different *model.* In some cases, the model is obvious, as in the regression approach where a formal mathematical equation model is made explicit. In other cases, the model is somewhat implicit, as in the market potential approach where the underlying model relates to the consumption behavior of families in distributing their income over various categories of purchases.

Each model requires different sets of information. In some cases, these *information sets* are partly the same for two models (e.g., several of the models require income data), but in general, *each model prescribes an information set.*

In Chapter 2, we described the concept of the value of information and delineated a number of characteristics of information for assessing its value (e.g., timeliness, relevance). Here, we see that *information has value with respect to a particular decision model.* Since the ultimate criterion for evaluating information is *usefulness* (see Figure 2-1), information is useful only in terms of the role that it plays in decision making. A first approximation to this is the model, explicit or implicit, which guides the decision process.

For instance, data on the number of families in each income category play an important role in the market potential model (Table 3-1) and no role at all in any of the other models. This is so despite the fact that the same broad concepts about income and consumption levels are used in many of the other models. Thus, this particular data element has value for the market potential model, but no value for the others.

This is merely another way of saying the obvious: data and information are valuable only if they are used. Since a model prescribes a way in which information may be used in a decision situation, the model largely determines the value of the information. Thus, the model, whether it be of the explicit variety or a mental model, is a key factor in determining the value of information.

Models as Definers of Information Requirements

The idea of information requirements is a pervasive one in information systems. Designers of information systems are always greatly concerned with defining and delineating the information requirements of the system's potential users. This is the basic definition of the work that is to be done by the system, the information that it is to provide.

Various approaches to the delineation of information requirements have been used by information system designers. These approaches range from the *inventory* approach, in which the data that the organization currently collects and uses are inventoried and it is assumed that this inventory represents requirements, to the approach in which managers are asked to list that information that they *need* or require.

Neither of these approaches explicitly takes into account the basic relationship between models and information and the opportunities that this relationship presents for assessing information requirements. We shall go into this in some detail in a later chapter on MMIS design. For now, we shall be satisfied to identify those specific model elements which prescribe information requirements and to suggest, by example, some of the ways in which models may be used to determine the information requirements of managers.

There are four primary model elements which serve to define information requirements: the model's predictive variables, its criterion variables, its solution, and sensitivity information associated with the solution.[7]

To understand how these various model elements prescribe information requirements, one must recognize that every problem situation may be described in terms of *various* alternative models. Every manager would probably develop a slightly different model to describe a given problem. Successful managers in similar situations probably have models that have a great deal in common, but since the model is an abstraction which describes the salient properties of a problem situation, it is clear that judgment determines the most appropriate model.

---

[7] Portions of this discussion are adapted with permission from William R. King and David I. Cleland, "Manager-Analyst Teamwork in MIS," *Business Horizons,* April 1971.

Predictor variables and
information requirements

A hypothetical manager-analyst discussion concerning the mental model which is used by the manager in addressing the previously discussed marketing expansion problem may be used to describe how the model's predictor variables may be analyzed to prescribe information requirements. Such a discussion serves, as well, to illustrate the various models or various degrees of abstract thinking which managers go through in assessing such a problem. It also suggests a useful process for information systems design which we shall go into further in Chapter 8.

The analyst might begin by asking the manager how he goes about evaluating a potential area in terms of his past experience with the product, similar products, and similar marketing situations. Suppose the manager responds by saying that because of market survey results and the product's price, he knows that the product appeals to the affluent. Therefore, he says, "We should try to sell it in the most affluent markets where it will obviously do best." The analyst concludes that perhaps expansion markets could be selected on the basis of the mean annual income of the market population or on some buying power index. This level of abstraction is described as Model 1 in Table 3-4.

Then the manager says, "Well, it isn't quite that simple, since the competition which we face in an area is important too. We feel that it's more difficult to enter an area in which a number of competitors are already entrenched than it is to enter an area where only a few competitors are selling their products."

TABLE 3-4 Factors Incorporated into Three Alternative Marketing Expansion Models

	Criterion	Predictive Factor	Measurement of Predictor
Model 1	Product success	Population affluence	Median annual income
Model 2	Product success	Population affluence Competition	Median annual income Number of competitors or market share of largest competitor
Model 3	Product success	Population affluence Competition	Median annual income Number of competitors or market share of largest competitor
		Population background or language capability	Percentage of foreign born Percentage of English- speaking

"Perhaps," thinks the analyst, "we can quantitatively assess this factor by simply using the number of competitors in the market or the market share of the largest competitor." While he is thinking, the manager says, "We have another problem. Whenever we've gone into an area like San Antonio, which has a large foreign-born or non-English-speaking population, we've had difficulties. We think it is because they are just more conservative, don't generally react as well to new products, and are difficult to communicate with through advertising."

In this dialogue, we see that a number of different models have been suggested. The process would probably go on for some time, but we can view these three alternative models as described in Table 3-4. The first is a simple one in which product success could be predicted by the market population's affluence. The analyst complemented this with a possible quantitative measure of the predictor variable, median annual income. In the second model, the manager includes competition as a predictor, and the analyst suggests ways in which this factor might be measured. The third model includes either population background or language capability, or both.

The manager could have gone on to suggest other more comprehensive models and, as is usually the case, he probably would have gone so far that the model finally selected to be best would not have been the one which was most comprehensive. Usually, in such a process, factors will be considered and then dropped as not sufficiently significant to warrant inclusion. The analyst in the hypothetical dialogue was performing two key functions in this process: interacting with the manager in order to help him enumerate the salient factors, and trying to suggest quantifiable measures of the factors.

Hence, one of the basic ways in which a model prescribes information requirements is in terms of the specification of the predictors and the measures which will be used to assess them. If Model 2 in Table 3-4 is finally selected to describe the decision problem, the predictor variables prescribe that the information system must produce information on mean annual incomes and market shares or number of competitors in each market.

The model criterion and information requirements

Another important aspect of the model—the criterion—also prescribes information. In the three models of Table 3-4, the implicit criterion involves the choice of markets to maximize product success. Of course, this aspect must also be operationalized; it might, for instance, be measured in terms of sales revenue. Thus, the criterion would be to choose those markets which are expected to produce the greatest sales. Alternatives are the market share measure or some measure which balances revenues with the significant costs of selling, say sales revenue dollars per promotional dollar. The criterion in these latter cases would be to choose as expansion markets those which can be expected to produce the greatest market share or the largest ratio of sales revenues to promotional expenses.

In each instance, the manager is considering various quantities to serve as a basis for his decision. He and the analyst jointly determine if a particular quantity is useful and can be measured and predicted. In doing so, they generate alternative models through a process of considering various criteria.

In one case of a marketing expansion decision, after it had been determined that quantitative measures of success could not be predicted, it was decided that a qualitative (good versus bad) measure be used as described earlier.[8] The manager and analyst jointly determined that the best practical model involved the comparison of potential areas with those areas which had been good for the product in the past and those which had been bad, and the selection of areas with characteristics most like good areas. Clearly, vastly different information requirements are prescribed if the criterion is maximization of sales revenues than if it is a qualitative comparison. In the latter case, the information system must be capable of accepting subjective inputs. The MMIS would then also be required to aggregate these subjective assessments according to prescribed rules. In the first case, the prescription of information requirements is much the same as with predictor variables—the specification of explicit numerical market data which must be incorporated into the data base.

The model solution and information requirements

If an optimization model, which prescribes a best action to be taken in a decision situation, is developed for a decision process, its solution may either prescribe important information requirements or constrain those already developed using the predicator variables and the criterion. For instance, one study which used the discriminant analysis approach to the solution of the marketing expansion problem [9] involved a solution which was obtained in the form of a simple *decision rule*. The decision rule specified that a prospective market area is to be considered more like past good areas than like past bad areas if a quantity calculated from the potential area's characteristics (income, number of competitors, and so on) is numerically greater than a prescribed cost ratio.

Symbolically, if k is the quantity calculated from the area characteristics, the decision rule is

[8] William R. King, "Toward a Methodology of Market Analysis," *Journal of Marketing Research*, August 1965.

[9] William R. King, "Marketing Expansion: A Statistical Analysis," *Management Science*, July 1963.

$$k \rangle \frac{C_1}{C_2}$$

where C_1 is the cost of predicting as bad an area that is actually good, and C_2 is the cost of predicting as good an area that is actually bad. If the reverse inequality holds, the complete decision rule specifies that the potential area be considered more like past bad areas than like good ones.

The critical informational aspect of the solution, the decision rule, *is that the relevant costs appear as a ratio.* Thus, the solution shows that the two costs do not need to be assessed separately in order to use the model. Only the ratio need be determined. The significance of this becomes apparent when one considers the difficulty in assessing these costs on an accounting basis. One is an *opportunity cost,* since if a good area is predicted as bad, a profit opportunity is lost. The other cost is that of selling the product in an area which turns out to be bad. Both would be difficult to assess separately. However, the two costs may be subjectively assessed as a ratio. Executives may be asked, Is it twice as costly to predict a good area as bad as it is to predict a bad area as good? Is it one-half as costly? They can, in this way, consider all the various implications which transcend accounting costs. For instance, what will be the effect on the firm's reputation?

Sensitivity information and information requirements

Models prescribe information requirements in a fourth way in terms of sensitivity information. This information simply tells the manager how sensitive the solution is to changes in various input quantities. For example, if the mean annual income in an area is expected to increase by $100 next year, how would the solution to the model change? If our estimate of the number of competitors in an area is inaccurate, how does this change the answer that the model has given us? Such information is a natural by-product of analytic models. As such, it is a useful variety of information for the manager and should be formally incorporated into the MMIS.

The importance of sensitivity information is illustrated in Figure 3-3, which shows a common situation in which the total cost of some activity is expressed in terms of a decision variable X. The curve depicted in that figure is a graphic cost model which might represent the total cost associated with different order quantities to be placed by a wholesaler.[10]

The objective of a model such as that shown in Figure 3-3 is the determination of the best, or optimal, value of the decision variable, X. This best, or least-

[10] For some simple approaches to such decision problems, see, for instance, Martin K. Starr and I. Stein, *The Practice of Management Science* (Englewood Cliffs, N.J.: Prentice-Hall, 1976).

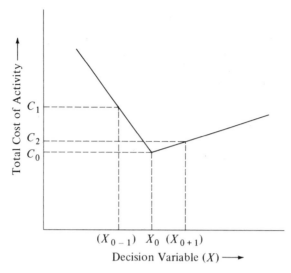

FIGURE 3-3 Determining optimal value of decision variable

cost value of X can be seen as X_0 in the figure, since that is the value of X for which the total cost is lowest.

Sensitivity information which can be associated with this optimal solution tells the decision maker something about the impact of deviating from the optimum value of the decision variable. For instance, as can be seen in Figure 3-3, it is much more costly to deviate below X_0 than above it. This is so because of the steepness of the total cost curve to the left of X_0 and the relatively less steep slope of the curve to the right of X_0. This can be seen by noting that the increase in total cost associated with moving from X_0 to $(X_0 - 1)$ is roughly five times the cost increase associated with a move from X_0 to $(X_0 + 1)$. This cost increase is from C_0 to C_1 in the former case and from C_0 to C_2 in the latter.

Such sensitivity information may be very valuable to the decision maker. If he cannot actually adopt the specified optimal value, X_0, because of some practical constraint, say because it involves fractional units or because he must order in carload lots, sensitivity information tells him the least cost direction in which to err. Such information can also suggest practical actions to be taken if he feels that some of the estimates which went into the development of the model may be in error, say, the unit costs which are used to develop the total cost expression.

Summary

Most decision problems may be addressed using a variety of different approaches, each of which involves some variety of a model, be it explicit or implicit. There even is a wide variety of sensible explicit models which can be applied in any given situation.

Each possible model prescribes a different set of information requirements which are necessary if the model is to be used effectively. Thus, since information is valued in terms of its usefulness, its value is relative to a particular model, or set of models, from which a requirement for specific information is generated. Of course, this is only a first approximation to developing operational measures for informational value, because a model (particularly the explicit kind) is only an approximation to the real decision problem. Thus, information may be used in making a decision in addition to that which is prescribed by the decision model. However, the model does provide a rigorous basis for beginning to develop measures of information values and define information requirements in ways that are useful for MMIS design.

Models serve to define information requirements in several specific ways in terms of their predictor variables, criterion, solution, and the sensitivity information which is associated with the solution. Each of these categories of information may be explicitly assessed in order to determine the useful, and hence valuable, information which is prescribed by the model.

EXERCISES

1. What are the advantages and disadvantages of the marketing potential approach to the problem of marketing expansion in terms of the cost of information and of the value-of-information criteria spelled out at the end of Chapter 2?

2. Evaluate each of the other approaches (cross-classification, simple regression, multiple criteria, multiple regression, and discriminant) in the same fashion.

3. Explain what it means to say that sales are positively related to income levels. Does it mean, for example, that higher income created by a new plant being located in an area will result in higher sales?

4. The multiple criteria approach can be said to ignore interdependencies among the criteria. Can you explain what interdependent criteria are and, therefore, what this means?

5. Identify the underlying model (set of relationships) for each of the six approaches to the marketing expansion problem. Then show how each model prescribes a specific set of required information.

6. Why might an inventory approach, in which the information that an organization collects is extensively inventoried, be a poor way to establish the organization's information requirements?

7. How might one go about evaluating the merits of the three models shown in Table 3-4 in terms of information cost-value?

8. What would be the implications of the cost-value information for each of the models in Table 3-4 in the case where product success is measured by the following:
   a. Sales level
   b. Good versus bad
   c. Sales, market share, and profitability

9. Can you think of ways, other than those illustrated in the text, in which the form of the *solution* to a model might affect the information requirements previously established in terms of the predictor variables and the criterion?

10. How can sensitivity analyses, such as that conducted in Figure 3-3, be used to assess the impact of errors in the model on the *actual* outcome of a decision situation? Construct an example in terms of Figure 3-3 to show this.

REFERENCES

Bruns, W. J., Jr. "Accounting Information and Decision-Making: Some Behavioral Hypotheses." *Accounting Review,* July 1968.

Comer, J. M. "Allocate: A Computer Model for Sales Territory Planning." *Decision Sciences,* July 1974.

Daniel, D. R. "Management Information Crisis." *Harvard Business Review,* 39 (September–October 1961).

DeCarbonnel, Francois E., and Dorrance, Roy G. "Information Sources for Planning Decisions." *California Management Review,* XV (Summer 1973):42–53.

Hess, Sidney W. "The Use of Models in Marketing Timing Decisions." *Operations Research,* July–August 1967.

Little, J. D. C., and Lodish, L. M. "A Media Planning Calculus." *Operations Research,* January–February 1969.

Lodish, L. M. "A 'Vaguely Right' Approach to Sales Force Allocations." *Harvard Business Review,* January–February 1974.

Mock, T. J.; Estrin, T. L.; and Vasarhelyi, M. A. "Learning Patterns, Decision Approaches, and the Value of Information." *Journal of Accounting Research,* Spring 1972.

Montgomery, David B. "The Outlook for MIS." *Journal of Advertising Research,* June 1973.

Munro, M. C. and Davis, G. B. "Determining Management Information Needs: A Comparison of Methods." Management Information System Research Center, MISRC-WP-75-04, University of Minnesota, Dec. 1974.

Schewe, Charles D. "Management Information Systems in Marketing: A Promise Not Yet Realized." *Management Informatics* 3 (1974).

Vazsonyi, A. "Information Systems in Management Science." *Interfaces,* May 1973, pp. 30–33.

4

The Structure of the MMIS

In this chapter, we turn our attention to the *system* which is to provide information to support marketing decision making. In Chapter 2, it was argued that the diverse and complex informational needs of marketing managers can best be met through the development of an MMIS, whether or not the system is computerized.

In this chapter various dimensions of the structure of the MMIS are depicted from a number of different points of view. This will lead to a better understanding of what an MMIS is all about and will also prove valuable in developing ways to design, develop, and use an MMIS more effectively.

Conceptual Structure of the MMIS

Figure 4-1 shows the conceptual structure of an information system as adapted from Marschak.[1] It shows a rather formalized information-oriented decision process which involves a cycle of inquiry into real-world events, encoding, transmission, decoding, and, ultimately, a decision situation resulting in the choice of a specific course of action. The chosen action impinges on the world, producing events which are again inquired into. Once observed, these events are translated into symbolic representations, which are then transmitted, decoded, and used to support another round of decision making.

The information system structure which is implicit in Figure 4-1 involves three major information subsystems: an (1) inquiring subsystem, a (2) transmission subsystem, and a (3) decision subsystem. In addition, there are subsidiary subsystems for encoding, decoding, etc.

The *inquiring subsystem* may be of many different varieties. For instance, a system in which basic data are recorded on forms by field salespeople represents a simple data capture system. A more sophisticated variety is represented by computer-linked point-of-sale devices which capture data that are punched in by the salesperson. Still a more advanced inquiry system is that which reads codes on grocery items or on the price tags of apparel and inputs these data into a computerized processing system which can automatically update inventory records.

Another variety of inquiry system might involve *random sampling,* the observation of a randomly chosen subset of the overall population of items on which decisions are to be based. Such an inquiry system would not be appropriate for determining a shopper's total purchase, but it is appropriate for assessing the proportion of spoiled, defective, or obsolete items in an inventory, for example. Such an inquiry approach is also useful in assessing consumer or customer opinions and preferences, much in the fashion of political polls.

[1] J. Marschak, "Economics of Inquiring, Communicating, Deciding," *Papers and Proceedings of the 18th Annual Meeting of the American Economics Association, American Economic Review,* May 1968.

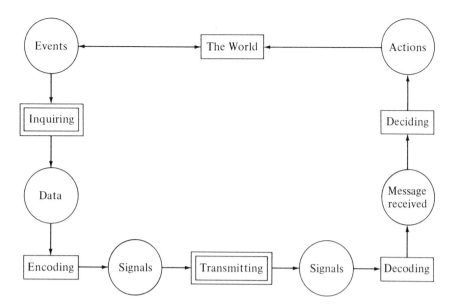

FIGURE 4-1 Conceptual structure of an information system

The *transmission subsystem* may also take varied forms. The passing of a report from the hand of the salesperson to the desk of the sales manager and personal phone calls are simple communications links. Data transmission over phone lines or other telecommunications channels, such as those routinely performed on a daily basis for reporting sales data from field offices to a central location is another level of transmission system.

The *decision subsystem* may be rather unsystematic, as in organizations where managers rely totally on subjective judgment based on information contained in reports presented to them. However, even in such unsystematic decision situations, the design of reporting forms, the information content of forms, the determination of reporting cycles, etc., are all elements of the decision support system. In more sophisticated decision support systems, sophisticated computerized models may serve the decision maker.

It is important to recognize that *every management information system must involve all three of these major subsystems,* although specific subsystems may be more important in one MMIS than in another. For instance, an MMIS which is oriented toward competitive intelligence gathering may emphasize the *inquiring* subsystem in that the major design elements concentrate on *where* and *how* to obtain information. Conversely, a system which has the primary feature of reporting sales from remote locations on a daily basis to a central office may emphasize the *transmission* subsystem in utilizing telecommunications data to achieve the reporting objective. Other systems involve decision models and, thereby, emphasize the *decision* subsystem.

Hierarchical Structure of the MMIS

An MIS is often thought of as operating at three levels which are equally appropriate. As noted by a Conference Board research report which surveyed marketing applications of information systems,

> . . . there are three levels of MIS, determined roughly by their flexibility, complexity, and question-answering power: (1) data storage and retrieval systems; (2) systems for monitoring the results of business activity; and (3) model-based analytical systems for evaluating business alternatives.[2]

The data storage and retrieval system level is addressed to the collection and storage of data and to the providing of rapid access to the contents of data files and library indices. For instance, a competitively oriented MMIS subsystem which provided the capability to inquire into past histories of competitors' sales, profits, etc., would be at this level, as are most library systems which provide abstracts of documents when inquiries are made in terms of key words.

The monitoring system level is oriented toward the *timely* reporting of the operating results of the enterprise and, perhaps, its competitors as well. These are the control-oriented systems which provide updated reports of production, sales, expenses, etc., and thereby give managers an opportunity to take action to rectify problems or to inquire further into the causes of poor performance.

The analytical systems level is oriented toward aiding in understanding the causes of problems or of prospects for the future through the incorporation of analytical models into the system. It is this latter most sophisticated level of MMIS toward which much of this book is focused, although because such systems are hierarchical in nature, the existence of the highest analytically oriented system level presumes that some variety of the lower-level systems also exists.

This analytical variety of MMIS which is the focus of this book might well be alternatively called either a marketing management decision support system or a marketing management decision and information system. These terms are frequently used to distinguish decision-oriented systems which are truly *management* information systems from those systems oriented to data processing which have been given the more sophisticated appellation MIS.

[2] S. J. Pokempner, "Information Systems for Sales and Marketing Management," Conference Board Report No. 591 (1973), p. i.

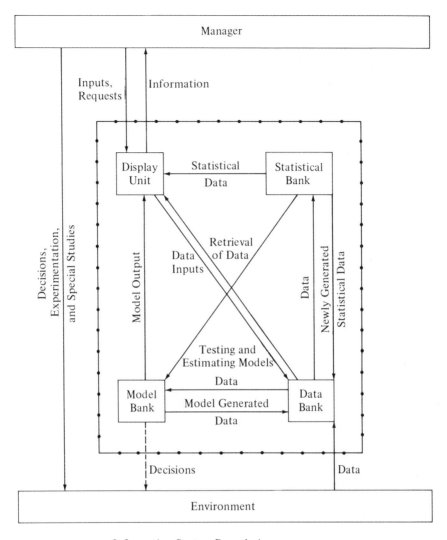

Information System Boundaries ━━●━━●━━

FIGURE 4-2 Structure of the decision information system

System Structure of the MMIS

A useful outline of an MMIS structure has been given, using the "decision and information system" nomenclature, by Montgomery and Urban.[3] Figure 4-2 is a diagram representing this decision-oriented variety of MMIS. It shows the sys-

[3] Adapted with permission from D. B. Montgomery and G. L. Urban, "Marketing Decision-Information Systems: An Emerging View," *Journal of Marketing Research,* published by the American Marketing Association, May 1970.

tem to consist of four primary interrelated elements which perform various functions between the manager and the environment in which he is operating. The four primary MMIS elements are (1) a data bank, (2) a measurement-statistics model bank, (3) a decision model bank, and (4) a display unit.

The data bank, or data base, is the medium for the storage of information which is deemed to be relevant to marketing activities and decisions. The information in the data bank may be processed through either or both of the measurement-statistics model bank and the decision model bank to produce information which is more refined and focused toward a specific use. The measurement-statistics bank consists of *data analysis models* varying from those which provide the capability to perform cross-classification analyses and calculate averages and variances to more sophisticated statistical analytic tools such as cluster analysis, regression analysis, and discriminant analysis. Basically, these varieties of analytic models represent the vehicles by which basic data are translated into value and likelihood information in the fashion discussed in Chapter 2.

The decision model bank entails models of specific decision problems. Illustrative of these are models for determining optimal advertising mixes, models for new product choice, and comprehensive simulation models of products, product lines, or businesses.

The measurement-statistics model bank and the decision model bank interact to some degree since statistical techniques may be used to estimate the parameters of decision models and to assess their validity.

The display unit is the device which facilitates manager interaction with the MMIS. The user-MMIS interface which the display unit represents may permit direct interaction between the manager and the system or it may permit communications only through intermediaries. It may be of widely differing forms depending on the needs and level of sophistication of the system's manager-users.

Input-Output Structure of the MMIS

Another way of looking at the MMIS structure is from the input-output standpoint. What information is collected and input into the system and how is it used?

Table 4-1 [4] does this in terms of a series of subsystems, listed in the middle column, which serve to relate *information sources* to *information uses*. As such it describes an MMIS structure in terms of inputs, outputs, and the subsystems which serve to facilitate the transformation of informational inputs into decision outputs.

[4] This table is adapted from a paper by the author, William R. King, and David I. Cleland: "Environmental Information Systems for Strategic Marketing Planning," *Journal of Marketing*, October 1974.

TABLE 4-1 Input-Output Subsystem Structure of the MMIS

Information Uses (Outputs)	Subsystems	Information Sources (Inputs)
1. Situation assessment (What is the current situation?)	Internal operations Customers Image	Internal Present customers Other external sources (economic, technological, etc.)
2. Goal development (What do we want the future situation to be?)	Potential customers Goals and policies	Potential customers Internal sources
3. Constraint identification (What constraints might inhibit us?)	Competition Regulatory	Competitors Government Other external sources
4. Selection of strategies (What shall we do to achieve our goals?)	Forecasting Cost-benefit Intelligence	Internal sources External sources

The uses of marketing information are specified in the left column of Table 4-1 in terms of the four critical questions which must be answered in any important choice situation. These questions are concerned with assessing the current situation, deciding what goals are to be sought, identifying the factors that may inhibit the achievement of the goals, and finally, the selection of a strategy to pursue the goals.

The information sources in the right column of Table 4-1 are not exhaustive; nor are they uniquely identified with the uses with which they are matched in the left column. However, there is a general tendency for them to be so related. For instance, most companys' assessments of the current situation will be focused on internal and customer sources of information. This is so because the company and its customers are the prime determinants of the current situation. Similarly, competitors and various government levels and agencies provide the most significant constraints on action in the form of competitive actions such as price cuts and the set of laws and government regulations within which business must be conducted; as such, these information sources primarily relate to constraint identification (number 3).

The subsystem structure which is outlined in the middle column of Table 4-1 is suggestive of the way in which an information system may be structured to collect and analyze the informational inputs in ways that will usefully support the decision outputs. For instance, the internal information which is useful for assessing the existing situation is primarily provided by the internal operating (transaction processing) and management control subsystems. Other information, for example, that concerning intangibles like the image of the organization as perceived by its customers, may be provided by an image subsystem.

Table 4-1 also shows that information on the goals to be sought comes from potential customers through a potential-customer subsystem and from internal sources through a goals and policies subsystem.[5] This latter subsystem treats the goals of the organization—that is, the subjective aspect inherent in all decision making—and the policies which serve to guide and constrain choice.

Constraint identification is similarly supported by subsystems dealing with the competitive and regulatory environments which create the most significant limitations on action. The final choice of a strategy is supported by a forecasting subsystem and cost-benefit subsystem, which are supported by internal and external sources. These subsystems aid in the overall assessment of the worth of proposed strategies and in the assessment of the risks which are inherent in each.

Finally, in the choice of a strategy, the management must be aware of specific occurrences in the competitive marketplace. Has the competition just raised their price? Are they likely to be introducing a new product in our product line next month? The answers to these specific questions can be obtained and processed through an intelligence subsystem.

Understanding Various Structural Concepts of the MMIS [6]

The reader should recognize that structural descriptions such as that provided by the decision-information structure of Figure 4-2 are sophisticated ones. Few organizations have implemented such systems in comprehensive form; yet many are proceeding toward such a goal and some have achieved it to a limited degree.[7]

The diagram of Figure 4-3 is a good device for understanding the various kinds of MMIS at various levels of sophistication that an organization might wish to develop.

Figure 4-3 shows a decision process which is expressed in information-oriented terms. It shows data being generated, collected into a data base, and processed through predictive and decision models. The overall result of the decision process is an action which is taken as the result of a choice made by a decision maker.

The models which comprise this process simply reflect the inherent necessity

---

[5] This and other subsystems introduced here are described in a later chapter.

[6] Parts of this section are adapted from William R. King and David I. Cleland, "Manager-Analyst Teamwork in MIS," *Business Horizons,* April 1971.

[7] For a description of the state of the art in such systems, see, for example, Liam Fahey, "Environmental Scanning: Its Conceptualization and Implementation in Twelve Large Corporations," University of Pittsburgh, Graduate School of Business, Working Paper 167 (1976).

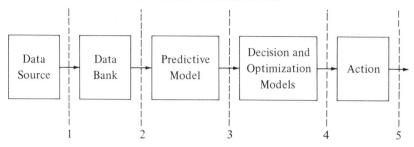

FIGURE 4-3 Decision process

SOURCE: Adapted from Richard O. Mason, Jr., "Basic Concepts for Designing Management Information Systems," AIS Research Paper No. 8, Graduate School of Administration, UCLA, October 1969.

for prediction and choice in any decision process. Predictive models are used to predict future events; decision models focus on specific choices; optimization models are a particular kind of decision model which specify the best course of action from among the available alternatives. Thus, a formal predictive model might result in sales forecasts, while a linear programming refinery model which produces the best production plan is an optimization model.

Of course, the decision process shown in the figure is a generic one, so that it does not require that these predictive and choice activities be conducted formally with explicit models. This point is made clear by considering the various *alternative system concepts* delineated by the various vertical dotted lines in Figure 4-3.

These vertical dotted lines represent different feasible man-machine system interfaces. In the case of each possible interface, the machine system is presumed to occupy those activities to the left of the interface, and the manager is presumed to deal with those to the right. For instance, if the man-machine system interface of a particular MMIS is at situation 1 in the figure, the MMIS is simply an information collection system; all data and models used in the decision process are stored in the mind of the manager. In other words, all models are mental models of the variety discussed in Chapter 2.

On the other hand, if the man-machine interface is at situation 2 in the figure, the data base is a part of the machine system, but all real decision-making mechanisms are handled by the manager. He is simply provided with reports which summarize and aggregate data. In situation 3, the manager also is provided with the output of predictive models, such as sales forecasts and forecasts of GNP. In situation 4, the manager is provided with the recommended courses of action as determined by decision models which may be of the optimization variety, that is, models which produce an answer, or recommended course of action for the decision maker. He might, for instance, be provided with the new product opportunity which is selected as best according to some criterion from among a set of available opportunities. He could then evaluate this recommendation in the light of his knowledge of the model and of those things which the model omits. In the last situation, 5, we have automated decision making, since the machine system even goes so far as to perform the action. Although this latter interface appears to be of the science fiction variety, systems do exist today which perform at this level for routine levels of decision making; for instance, systems which monitor stock levels and print up purchase requisitions (action) on an automatic basis when minimum allowable levels are reached.

Figure 4-3 permits analysis of various viewpoints of the "proper" structure of an MMIS. Two extreme positions on the role of models in an MMIS will define the problems involved. First, the data processing expert might say that models, aside from simple accounting procedure models, have a minor role in an MMIS. Their role is to use information generated by the MMIS to analyze decisions. He might argue that most complex strategic decisions cannot be solved with formal mathematical models; rather, they must be dealt with on the basis of the judgment, experience, and intuition of an informed manager. The providing of information to the manager is the task of the MMIS.

The other extreme is the position of the management scientist, who might take the position that mathematical models are an intrinsic part of any modern MMIS. He might argue that all decisions cannot be left to managers, since decisions which involve many alternatives, and in which the objective is rather clear, can be more efficiently solved by a computerized model. For example, the manager of an oil refinery would find it impossible to consider each of the myriad of alternative production plans without the aid of linear programming models.

The resolution of these extreme positions is simple. If one accepts the premise of a decision-oriented MMIS, both of these positions are correct! *A modern sophisticated MMIS should allow for all varieties of model utilization from the most formal to the most subjective and informal.* Thus, a modern MMIS can involve routinely collected information that is processed and used to exercise models, such as sales data collected through point-of-sale terminals automatically used to adjust stock levels and to exercise reorder models. Such a system may also encompass ad hoc information about a competitor which is verbally reported to a designated individual and matched with other similar reports in order that intelligence "guesstimates" about competitors may be made. In the former case, the model is a formal part of the system; in the latter, the model exists primarily in the minds of the participants. However, both are potentially worthwhile to the organization, and both can be systematized through their incorporation into an overall MMIS design.

It should also be noted that it is common practice to use the term management information system to describe systems which have their sole or major interface at 2, 3, 4, and sometimes even 5 in Figure 4-3. (Seldom does anyone use the term to describe situation 1.) Thus, two people may find themselves agreeing on MMIS procedures, only to find that they are each using different MMIS definitions, depending on their own concept of the interface.

Relating the MMIS structure to MMIS concepts

An understanding of the relationships between Figures 4-2 and 4-3 can be enlightening. Figure 4-2 depicts a system structure in operational terms; that is, in terms of specific entities such as data banks, model banks, etc., which it contains. Figure 4-3 is conceptual in nature and shows various concepts of an MMIS in terms of man-machine interfaces. However, the two are quite consistent.

The operational system of Figure 4-2 represents a structure reflecting the system level of situation 4, or perhaps even 5, of Figure 4-3. This is because the measurement-statistics model bank involves models of the predictive variety while the decision model bank involves models of the decision and optimization variety. Since both are included in the MMIS structure in Figure 4-2, the system represents at least a level of situation 4; that is, both predictions and decision analysis are being performed within the system rather than by the manager.

If only the measurement-statistics model bank, and not the decision model bank, had been incorporated into the MMIS structure of Figure 4-2, the system would be of the level 3 variety since only predictions, and not decision analyses, can be performed by the measurement-statistics model bank. Similarly, if neither of the model banks had been incorporated, the system would be of the level 2 variety in Figure 4-3.

Summary

All information systems encompass the basic functions of inquiring, transmitting, and deciding, although specific systems may emphasize these three subsystems to varying degrees. Clearly, a data storage and retrieval system emphasizes the inquiring and transmission subsystems. A system which is oriented to the monitoring of the results of business activity devotes greater attention to the transmission subsystem, while a model-based analytical system emphasizes the decision subsystem.

An MMIS which is of the decision-oriented variety may be structured to include a data bank, a measurement-statistics model bank, a decision model bank, and a display unit. These elements process both internal and external information for the support of various functions, such as marketing research, product and market planning, advertising and sales promotion, field sales and customer service.

One way of conceptualizing these input-output structural relationships is in terms of subsystems which service these various functions, or in terms of subsystems which support various phases of the planning and control process. For instance, certain subsystems are specifically oriented to the support of management choice processes.

The various kinds of systems which are referred to under the broad MIS acronym may be better understood in terms of a comparison between the degree to which models are incorporated into the system (the nonhuman part of the system) and the degree to which such models are expected to reside within the mind of the system's user-manager. Systems which differ greatly in this respect are often grouped into the broad MIS category. However, the most useful MMIS will itself incorporate a wide variety of subsystems that are different in this respect; for example, some MMIS subsystems operating at the level of data processing to support the mental models of managers and others incorporating models into the subsystem to provide the manager with recommended actions rather than just with information, as the layman might define it.

EXERCISES

1. The inquiry and transmission subsystems are not generally of great concern in a non-marketing MIS. Can you explain why this is so? Why are they so important in a marketing MIS?

2. Starting with each marketing decision illustration below, describe what the overall system of Figure 4-1 might look like. In other words what form might the inquiring subsystem take? the transmitting subsystem? the deciding subsystem? What would the form of the signals and messages be? What are the events and actions?
   a. Pricing decision
   b. Media-mix decision
   c. Individual credit decision
   d. Choice of a new marketing vice-president

3. What constitutes the inquiry, communications, and decisions subsystems in each of the following?
   a. Library retrieval system
   b. Billing system for credit card customers
   c. Computerized medical diagnosis system in which the patient is "hooked up" to the computer and a diagnosis is provided by the system

4. How might Montgomery and Urban's system, as described in Figure 4-2, be applied to the marketing expansion decision situation of Chapter 3 for each of the six approaches described in that chapter? In other words, for each approach, what

would the data bank contain, what would the decision model bank contain, and what would the statistical bank contain?

5. Why might a company want to have an MMIS image subsystem? What information do you think such a subsystem would contain?

6. Try to specify what you think each of the subsystems listed in Table 4-1 would contain. What sort of data would be input? What outputs would be provided? To whom would these output be useful?

7. Categorize the following kinds of systems in terms of the various man-machine interfaces of Figure 4-3.
   a. data processing system
   b. linear programming oil refinery scheduling system
   c. forecasting system
   d. library document retrieval system

REFERENCES

Ackoff, R. L. "Toward a Behavioral Theory of Communications." *Management Science,* April 1958.

Aguilar, Francis Joseph. *Scanning the Business Environment.* New York: Macmillan, 1976.

Baughman, James P.; Lodge, George C.; and Pifer, Howard W. *Environmental Analysis for Management.* Homewood, Ill.: Irwin, 1974.

Cleland, D. I., and King, W. R. "Competitive Business Intelligence Systems." *Business Horizons,* December 1975.

Coe, T. L. "Allocating the Corporate Information Processing Resource." *Journal of Systems Management,* August 1974, pp. 18–22.

Emery, J. C. "An Overview of Management Information Systems." *Data Base,* Winter 1973, pp. 1–15.

Gorry, G. A., and Scott Morton, M. S. "A Framework for Management Information Systems." *Sloan Management Review,* Fall 1971, pp. 55–70.

Kashyap, R. N. "Management Information Systems for Corporate Planning and Control." *Long Range Planning,* June 1972.

Kelley, William T. "Marketing Intelligence for Top Management." *Journal of Marketing* 29 (October 1965): 19–24.

King, William R., and Cleland, David I. "Environment Information Systems for Strategic Marketing Planning." *Journal of Marketing* 38 (October 1974): 35–40.

———. "Decision and Information Systems for Strategic Planning." *Business Horizons,* April 1973.

Kotler, Philip. "A Design for the Firm's Marketing Nerve Center." *Business Horizons* 9 (Fall 1966): 63–74.

Mandell, S. L. "The Management Information System Is Going to Pieces." *California Management Review,* Summer 1975, pp. 50–56.

Marschak, J. "Economics of Inquiring, Communicating, Deciding." *Papers and Pro-*

ceedings of the 18th Annual Meeting of the American Economics Association, American Economic Review, May 1968.

Thomas, Philip S. "Environmental Analysis for Corporate Planning." *Business Horizons,* October 1974.

———. "Marketing Intelligence Systems: A Dew Line for Marketing Men." *Business Management,* January 1966, pp. 32, 34, and 68.

5

MMIS Subsystems and Their Uses

Previous chapters have concentrated on conceptual outlines of the structure of the MMIS and on simple illustrations of marketing decisions and supporting marketing information. In this chapter, we elaborate on the MMIS in terms of the substantive content of various MMIS subsystems and the uses to which each subsystem may be put. The situations described in this chapter for each subsystem are taken from applications in the real world.

In describing both MMIS subsystems and the uses for the informational outputs of the various subsystems, we are emphasizing the intrinsic relationship between information and decision making—a point to which we shall return in subsequent chapters when we deal with MMIS design and development processes.

Obviously, it is impractical to exhaustively describe the myriad MMIS subsystems which may prove to be desirable for any particular organization and circumstance. The objective here is to delineate subsystems which have proved to be useful in real-world marketing management and to suggest areas of application for the MMIS which may not be apparent to the uninitiated.

It should be recognized at the outset that not all the subsystems to be devised need be computerized. Indeed, the various subsystems are extremely varied with regard to the volume of data which need be handled and the speed with which it need be provided to decision makers, as well as with regard to the nature of the data itself (numerical, alphabetical, etc.). Thus, some subsystems will require computers while some will not readily be amenable to computerization. But, each subsystem is a viable element in the overall MMIS, whether it involves masses of data, flashing computer lights, and whirling tapes or merely a designated individual to gather data, analyze them, and pass them on to those managers who can make use of them.

The various subsystems identified in Table 4-2 form the basis for the delineation of the substance and nature of MMIS subsystems in this chapter. These subsystems provide information on the following:

Internal operations

Customers

Image

Potential customers

Goals and policies

Competition

Regulatory factors

Forecasting

Cost-benefit assessment

Intelligence

Internal Operations Subsystem

The sophisticated decision-oriented subsystems which form the major focus for modern management information systems tend to overshadow the significance of the transaction processing and operational control system levels. However, the operating elements are essential to the MMIS, since it is important that accurate, up-to-date, operating information be available to marketing decision makers. No sophisticated system could exist without the underlying support of the operations subsystem; and even those subsystems which focus on entirely different substantive areas must usually have their output supplemented by information from the operations subsystem in order to be most useful.[1] For instance, a competitive MMIS subsystem which produces profiles of competitors in terms of sales volumes, geographic sales patterns, and sales promotional effort does not depend on the internal operations system for direct support. However, in order for this information about competition to be useful in decision support, it must be complemented with comparable internal information. By contrasting our sales distributions with that of our competitor by product and geographical area, and by comparing relative sales promotional expenditures, we can assess our strengths and weaknesses relative to competition.

Thus, while the internal operations subsystem, with its capability for processing order, inventory, and invoice information, is indeed a repository of data which are pertinent to management decision making, most operations systems are developed with decision support only as a secondary objective. Such subsystems generally need to be supplemented with customer-information subsystems in order that they be useful in decision support.

Customer Information Subsystem

Three varieties of customer information are of special significance for marketing decision support—individual customer, aggregate customer, and trend information. Thus, while relatively unsystematic data on individual customers may be sufficient to the salesperson for short-run tactical choices, broader-scale decisions require systematically collected and analyzed information on major customers as well as information on sets of customers who form identifiable market segments. Such segments are made up of groupings of customers who are homogeneous in some sense which is relevant to the decisions to be made. For example, an industrial market segment may be made up of customers who are similar with regard to industry, purchase behavior, or responses to the business cycle.

---

[1] The operations subsystem, as described here, should be distinguished from the operating programs discussed in Chapter 1. Operating programs direct a computer system in performing routine calculational functions. The operations subsystem is that portion of the overall system which processes transactional data.

Aggregate customer information

Consider the information in Table 5-1 for an illustration of one variety of output which a customer information subsystem can provide.[2] It shows aggregated information on customer market segments defined by annual volume as well as the profit contribution and selling cost for each segment.

The information contained in Table 5-1 represents the compilation of much basic data which must be collected, aggregated, and compiled from basic sales reports. When complemented with trend information on costs, profitability, and volumes, it represents basic decision support information for decisions on questions such as

What frequency of sales calls should be used for each segment?

How many salesmen do we need?

What is the best way to compensate salesmen so that the organization's overall objectives are best achieved?

For instance, the profit contribution per dollar of selling cost in the last column represents an aggregation of data that are processed by the internal operations subsystem. The calculation of this quantity requires that salespeople's wage payments be tabulated, that their expense reports be tabulated, and that their trip reports be analyzed (in order to determine with which customers they have spent their time). Moreover, data must be collected on all orders by each customer, and each customer must then be categorized by the appropriate range of annual account volume. Further, the different profit margins on the various products which may be sold to a given customer must be tabulated and aggregated into an average for each market segment.

This single useful variable, profit contribution per dollar of selling cost, is, thereby, created from data that exist within the internal operating subsystem, but clearly, the development of a computer output such as Table 5-1 requires a great deal of additional programming and analysis beyond the programs of the internal operations systems.

Analyses such as Table 5-1 are not normally output by operations systems, simply because they have been designed for transaction processing and operational control, not for decision support. Thus, a new subsystem, here termed a customer information subsystem, is necessary if the transactional data in the internal operations subsystem are to be useful for the support of management decisions.

This is made more evident when one realizes that even the information of

---

[2] Adapted with permission from Kurt H. Schaffir, "Marketing Information Systems," *Management Informatics,* vol. 3, no. 1 (February 1974), p. 31.

TABLE 5-1 Customer Information Output *

Annual Account Volume	Number of Accounts	Profit Contribution (000)	Contribution per Account	Selling Cost per Account	Contribution per Dollar of Selling Cost
$100,000+	500	$50,500	$101,000	$888	$118
$ 25,000–99,999	700	22,000	31,300	460	71
$ 15,000–24,999	1,100	7,800	7,000	240	29
$ 8,000–14,999	2,000	7,000	3,600	228	16
$ 4,000–7,999	2,900	5,000	1,700	226	8
$ 2,000–3,999	3,400	3,000	900	74	1
$ 1,000–1,999	3,100	1,200	400	76	5
Below 1,000	8,200	700	90	38	3
Total	21,900	$97,200			

* Adapted with permission from Schaffir, Kurt H., "Marketing Information Systems," *Management Informatics*, vol. 3, no. 1 (February 1974), p. 31.

83

Table 5-1 is but the *raw material* for decision support. These raw materials must be further processed and supplemented if they are to be directly useful.

Information on customer trends

Information such as that in Table 5-1 must be complemented with information on *trends* in order that it be useful in decisions such as those involving the best frequency of sales calls, number of salespeople and sales compensation programs. This is so because the data from which Table 5-1 was compiled represent the past, and the best sales strategy *for the future* must be determined from them.

Thus, the information of Table 5-1 must be complemented and adjusted by trend information such as whether various customer segments have been growing faster than others so that the distribution of sales across segments could reasonably be expected to be different next year than it was last year; whether the selling cost per account has been increasing and the proportional increase is different for various customer segments; whether customers in a given segment are changing their purchase patterns for various products so that the overall profitability per account is changing. Each of these items of *trend information* represents analyses of basic data which must be performed if intelligent decisions are to be made based on historical information. And each of these items of trend information must be obtained through analytic programs which operate on basic data produced by the internal operating subsystem.

This illustrates the need for a customer information subsystem that goes beyond the usual internal operations subsystem and also the need for the hierarchical nature of decision support systems. In discussing system structure in Chapter 4, we noted that systems which monitor the results of business activity and analytically oriented systems required data storage and retrieval systems for support. In the concept of an overall MMIS, the internal operations subsystem plays the role of a data storage and retrieval system on which more sophisticated systems can be built. The customer subsystem is one such sophisticated system. This is so despite the fact that it largely deals with the same data, namely customer data, as does the internal operations subsystem.

Customer profiles

Information on individual customers which goes beyond that usually contained in the operational level systems is also of great value to marketing managers. Now we shall illustrate the uses of customer profiles, as supplied by the customer information subsystem, in the development of sales goals for the coming year.

The table at the top of Figure 5-1 describes three departments—X, Y, and Z—in a customer organization. Note that this level of information is quite different from that which the usual transaction processing system would develop in

6	3	5	1	2	4
Plans for Next Year	Product Usage $ (000)	Factor	Department	Company Sales $ (000)	Share
(Increase from 10.0 to 10.5 Million Tons)					
Rebuild Unit	$ 200	.02	X	$ 12	6%
Add Capacity	300	.03	Y	210	70
	100	.01	Z	30	30
	$ 600	.06		$252	43%

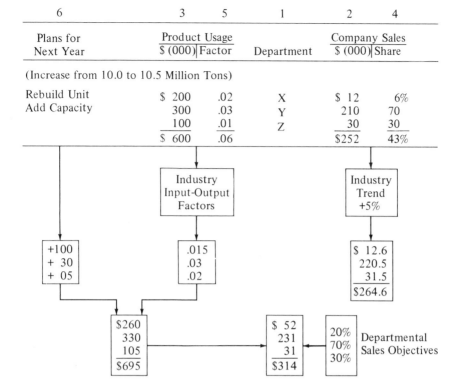

FIGURE 5-1 Customer profiles and managerial uses in establishing sales objectives

SOURCE: Adapted from Kurt H. Schaffir, "Marketing Information Systems," *Management Informatics*, vol. 3, no. 1 (February 1974), p. 31.

that it gives a profile of the customer in terms of the specific customer department to which our sales go, our share of the business of each department and our knowledge of the customer's overall and departmental plans for the coming year.

The calculations shown in boxes connected by arrows in the lower half of that figure represent the use of customer profile information in establishing our sales objective for that customer for the coming year. The software of the customer information subsystem may well perform many of these calculations routinely, or they may be performed by the manager depending on the nature of the system interface (as described in Figure 4-3).

Referring to the information in the table at the top of Figure 5-1, we see that column 1 designates the three departments X, Y, and Z and that column 2 shows last year's sales to each. When the total sales of $252,000 is transformed according to an industry trend of plus 5 percent for next year, these can be simply translated into expected sales of $264,600 as shown in the boxes below column 2.

However, a better estimate can be obtained through the use of more detailed information as contained in a customer profile. For instance, the data in column 3 show *total* usage of the product line by each department of the customer's firm, not just that product which is purchased from us. This shows, in column 4, that our firm had only 43 percent of the total product line sales in this firm last year. Moreover, column 4 shows that those sales were unevenly distributed proportionally among the three departments.

These data lead to the calculation, the results of which are shown in column 5, of the *product usage factor* of each customer department. This shows that department X uses 2 cents worth of our product per ton of its output while departments Y and Z use 3 cents and 1 cent per ton of output respectively (based on an output of 10 million tons for the customer firm).

Data such as those in column 5 can be supplemented with industry data, as shown in the industry input-output factors of Figure 5-1. These data reflect broader industry standards which will probably be reflected in new consumption patterns of this customer.

Column 6 shows the customer's plans for next year—to increase output from 10 million tons to 10.5 million tons. However, purchases of our product line are expected to increase disproportionately because department X plans to rebuild a unit, which is expected to add an incremental $100,000 in purchases, while department Y will add capacity and thus increase purchases by $30,000. Department Z's needs are expected to increase only in proportion to the overall industry trend of 5 percent.

The bottom left portion of Figure 5-1 shows how the industry input-output factors and information on the customer's plans for next year can be combined to obtain a total sales forecast of $695,000, based on a continuation of last year's overall sales effort.

However, we may not wish simply to continue the level of sales effort which was undertaken last year. Indeed, because of the disproportionately low share of the customer's business which we achieved in his department (X) last year, we might decide to undertake a major sales effort there to bring our share to 20 percent.

The right, bottom section of Figure 5-1 shows that departmental sales objectives for department X have been raised from a 12 percent to a 20 percent share for next year, while the share objectives for the other two departments remain the same.

When these objectives are combined with the forecasts at the left, they lead to an overall sales objective of $314,000 as shown at the bottom, middle of the figure. This contrasts with the estimate of $264,600 which might have been developed on the basis of less detailed information than that which is provided by the customer profile.

This example illustrates that the keys to creating customer information subsystems are two: first, new varieties of information in the form of levels of detail, aggregates, and trends; and second, a built-in analytic capability that permits the objective analysis of this customer information. Such a customer MMIS subsystem can serve to complement effectively the internal operations system so that the data processed in the organization's daily transactions become truly useful in the support of management decisions.

Image Information Subsystem

Another subsystem which provides crucial information concerning the current situation, the image subsystem, is based on the premise that the facts concerning objective information (costs, profits, sales, etc.) are not the sole, or best, descriptors of the existing situation.

Of course, objective information can be complemented with the subjective judgments of managers, but often the subjective judgments expressed within an organization reflect a degree of parochialism which can be very detrimental. Indeed, internal subjective judgments are often unduly influenced by the objective information available to managers, when the real value of such subjective information is as a complement to the hard facts, not merely as a mirror image of the objective information.

Most importantly, however, internally generated judgmental data do not provide critical information concerning the firm's external *image* as it is projected to, and perceived by, the customers and potential customers on whom the firm depends for its success.

Experience with industrial marketers suggests that there are great discrepancies between a firm's image of itself and the image held by its customers. Often these discrepancies are less significant in their impact on the firm's current operations than in terms of their potential impact in the future. For instance, the firm that sees itself as technically superior may find that its associated image of being high priced is more important to its future success.

A firm's image may be assessed in two general areas: product image (price, quality, reliability, etc.) and organizational image (quality of personnel, responsiveness, integrity, etc.). The basic techniques to use in the formal image survey in an industrial products situation are *structured and unstructured personal interviews* of key customer personnel. A questionnaire to serve as a guide for the conduct of these interviews can be developed and tested within the seller's organization. This in-house testing can be used as a basis to define and describe operationally the important dimensions of the product and the organizational characteristics that are deemed to be important to the seller's image. For example, in one such survey, the customer interviews centered around an evaluation of the following product and organization characteristics:

General characteristics

Personnel image

Ability to communicate with customers

Project management skills and capabilities

Ability to meet normal customer requirements

Responsiveness to customer's special requirements

Negotiating skills

Special capabilities

Product characteristics

The overall image that emerged in one such case was surprising to the executives of the sponsoring organization. It depicted an honest and technically competent organization that lacked marketing aggressiveness. This lack of aggressiveness was reflected in the customers' perceptions of virtually all aspects of customer contact, from the bureaucratic lack of responsiveness concerning customer inquiries to the lack of contact of top management with customers. Such specifics as the failure to communicate to customers about key personnel changes in the organization and deficiencies in the technical proposals presented to customers were also pointed out. The seller's products were rated high in terms of operating characteristics—performance, reliability, and ease of maintenance—but customers raised serious questions about the seller's overall capability to manage a technical product development effort and still maintain cost and schedule credibility.

The image survey was also conducted internally by querying personnel within the sponsoring company. The contrast between customer perceptions and internal personnel perceptions led management to take a number of specific actions designed to have a short-run impact on the image as well as to formalize the incorporation of image considerations into the planning activities of the firm. This led, for the first time, to specific concern with the image that the company wished to project and the actions that it could take to reach this image goal.

Such incorporations of image information as an integral and continuing part of the marketing planning process require that some type of formal information subsystem be established. In the case in point, the economic impracticality of continuing large-scale surveys led the firm to integrate the continuing image-monitoring activities into other information subsystems where image-related surrogate measures were monitored and assessed. In this firm, the overall image assessment is to be updated at two-year intervals.

Image assessment in a consumer product context can be conducted through a variety of means other than that of personal interviews. For instance, a mail survey or telephone survey can be used.[3] Table 5-2 shows the partial results of a telephone survey conducted by the Office of the Secretary of Defense [4] which was, in part, designed to permit the assessment of attitudes toward the military services (in this case, the Air Force). The entries represent the percentage of the sample group who associate each attribute with the Air Force in various geographic tracking areas. The circled entries represent those which differ significantly (on a statistical basis) from the overall U.S. percentage.

These data are routinely collected on a semiannual basis and compared and evaluated for trends and seasonal effects. The image evaluation is a continuing one, systematically conducted and utilized to assess marketing strategy in various areas of the country. Thus, what might be thought of by some as a marketing research study for a social product (military service) has become routinized and integrated into managerial decision processes to such a degree as to warrant being thought of as part of the organization's MMIS.

The data of Table 5-2 also serve to illustrate the pervasiveness of marketing concepts and information in today's world. As noted in Chapter 1, virtually every organization finds itself in the business of marketing, even the U.S. Department of Defense; and all face the need for developing marketing information for the support of decision making.

Potential-Customer Information Subsystems

While most organizations have some form of organized information about current customers, few have similar information on potential customers. Yet, such information is of equal importance for the development of strategic goals, since potential customers represent the opportunities that will ultimately determine the organization's future. Information on potential customers permits the organization to make rational choices concerning its future products, services, and markets.

The development of a potential customer information subsystem is not a straightforward task for most organizations. The list of potential customers is infinite, so some rational culling of this list must be performed. This can be started

[3] For a discussion of various survey techniques, see R. Ferber, *Marketing Research Handbook* (New York: McGraw-Hill, 1974), sec. II, pt. B.

[4] "Youth Attitude Tracking Study: Spring 1976." Report prepared for the U.S. Department of Defense by Market Facts, Inc., July 1976.

Imagery Attributes Most Associated with Air Force

Attribute (percent most associating attribute with Air Force)	Total U.S. (%)	NYC (%)	Alb. Buf. (%)	Hrsbg. (%)	D.C. (%)	FL (%)	AL MS TN (%)	OH (%)	MI IN (%)	Chic. (%)	MN NB ND SD (%)	TX (%)	So. CA (%)	No. CA (%)
Opportunity to better life	23.4	(14.2)	23.7	22.3	19.1	25.4	24.5	26.4	24.1	21.1	20.8	27.6	28.5	20.5
Trains for leadership	11.9	(5.8)	12.3	10.7	9.9	(17.0)	12.1	10.5	14.7	16.4	(4.4)	11.1	14.6	12.9
Teaches valuable trade	28.3	30.1	29.5	24.6	28.2	30.4	34.7	28.1	26.6	25.4	(17.7)	34.3	31.9	25.1
College education	20.7	(13.4)	19.9	21.7	(13.2)	22.4	24.0	25.5	20.8	(14.1)	17.8	(28.4)	20.8	24.8
See many countries	16.4	(24.5)	19.4	15.5	(11.1)	21.8	14.7	18.2	(7.5)	13.2	13.7	(23.6)	16.3	12.6
Good benefits for family	17.4	13.5	20.6	19.3	18.1	15.9	15.2	16.4	17.7	18.6	17.1	20.6	18.4	18.3
Career you can be proud of	22.6	(14.6)	21.3	24.7	18.8	24.0	(29.1)	22.6	(15.4)	20.2	(16.7)	25.7	28.3	27.5
Men you like to work with	17.5	(13.2)	14.4	15.7	16.6	14.6	19.1	16.5	17.8	10.7	14.4	24.6	21.5	16.7
Job you want	20.3	(6.8)	17.9	19.3	18.9	21.4	24.5	21.6	21.6	16.4	(12.7)	(26.9)	27.5	21.9
Challenging job	26.0	(14.7)	22.2	23.4	21.4	24.8	31.4	25.1	25.8	26.1	21.0	29.4	27.4	23.9
Pays well to start	16.3	(6.9)	13.6	14.7	17.3	15.5	(22.3)	17.1	16.9	16.9	(11.2)	21.3	15.1	17.3

Note: Circled entries are those where total U.S. falls beyond the range of two standard errors of the tracking area estimate.
Base: All respondents.

by using a criterion that reflects the potential of a particular segment of the overall market. For instance, one commercial bank determined that many small manufacturing firms (the initial criterion) in the local area could avail themselves of a variety of bank services. They began to construct a data base using commercially available services such as Dun & Bradstreet's *State Sales Guides* [5] and those provided by various manufacturers' associations. They then assessed the potential of various segments of the market (a more refined criterion) through personal contacts made on a test basis.

Another firm, after having built the data base and having identified high potential firms, developed a clipping service for collecting and assembling published references to these potential customers. A great deal of intelligence information concerning the plans of potential customers can be obtained in this way. When such information is made available to marketing planners and sales managers, they can use it in much the same way as that described for existing customers, for example, to identify prospects and establish sales objectives for them.

Goals and Policies Subsystem

The goals and policies subsystem is somewhat different from the other subsystems in both concept and nature. Most assuredly, such a subsystem is not of the variety that requires the manipulation of large amounts of data. Rather, it is addressed toward the providing of policy information to middle level managers to guide their decision making.

Although it is generally recognized that the values of top management, as indicated in organizational policies, must play an important role in all decisions, often these policies are left unclear in the minds of middle managers, who have usually not participated in their development. The result can be that inconsistent choices are made by various managers unfamiliar with the goals and policies that have been determined for the organization.

For instance, Ackoff [6] uses the term "stylistic objectives and constraints" to describe those nonquantifiable things that the organization has decided, as a matter of policy, it will or it will not do. He gives the following examples:

1. The company is not interested in any government-regulated business.
2. The businesses into which they may go must permit entry with modest initial investments but eventually permit large investments to be made.
3. The technology of any new businesses should be directly related to that used in current businesses.

[5] Published for various states by Dun and Bradstreet, Inc., New York, N.Y. 10008.
[6] R. L. Ackoff, *A Concept of Corporate Planning* (New York: Wiley, 1970), pp. 28–29.

A subsystem that provides a way to keep the ever-changing goals and policies at a high level of awareness in the minds of middle managers can simply be a manual or file containing updated versions of goals and policies categorized by various areas of activity (e.g., new products, credits, etc.) or it may be a more sophisticated retrieval system; but the existence of such a subsystem helps make sure that the choices made throughout the organization will be consistent with an overall plan.

Competition Subsystem [7]

Information about competition is potentially so important and voluminous that its collection, analysis, and use can consume a major part of a company's time and resources. A simple MMIS subsystem for information about competition focuses on providing a competition profile to managers in much the same way as a customer profile is provided (discussed earlier). However, competition profiles are usually less quantitative and specific, because the inquiry subsystem is not already tuned in to the competitor's organization, as it is to the customer's.

For instance, competitors who are identified to be outperforming one's own organization can be identified, and their significant actions and strategies can be cataloged and analyzed. Several major issues must be addressed with regard to competition:

First: Who are the several most threatening competitors?

Second: What are the strengths and weaknesses of the competition?

Third: What is believed to be the strategy (and associated risk postures) of the competition?

Fourth: What resources (financial, plant and equipment, managerial know-how, marketing resources, and technical capabilities) are at the competition's disposal to implement his strategies?

Fifth: Do any of these factors give the competition a distinctly favorable position?

Types of information about competition

Since a list of everything a business organization would like to know about a competitor would be almost endless, a representative list of what is required serves to illustrate the usefulness of such information. While the details needed

---

[7] Portions of this section are adapted from the author's paper with William R. King and colleague David I. Cleland: ''Competitive Business Intelligence Systems,'' *Business Horizons,* December 1975.

vary somewhat from company to company, there are basic elements required for most analyses about competition.

Marketing information

Pricing, discounts, terms, product specifications

Volume, history, trend, and outlook for a given product

Market share and trend

Marketing policies and plans

Relations with customers and image

Size and deployment of sales force

Channels, policies, and methods of distribution

Advertising expenditures in various media

Production and product information

Evaluation of quality and performance

Breadth of line

Processing and process technology

Product cost

Production capacity

Location and size of production facilities and distribution facilities

Packaging capabilities

Delivery record

Research and development capability

Organizational and financial information

Identification of key decision makers

Philosophies of key decision makers

Financial condition and outlook

Expansion and acquisition programs

Major problems and opportunities

Research and development programs

The competition subsystem is a good one for demonstrating the need for new and innovative kinds of systems that go beyond the scope of the usual operational marketing information system.[8] Such systems are needed for the following reasons:

[8] Such systems are often referred to as *business intelligence systems* although we are reserving the term *intelligence system* here to mean something different.

1. Competitive business information is essential for ensuring success in competing in a particular market.
2. Markets today are changing so dramatically that informal means of maintaining surveillance concerning competition are inadequate.
3. Reliance on hit or miss methods for obtaining such information is ineffective in the long run. A total *system* is required.
4. A competition information subsystem can be highly personalized even though it is rigorously organized and operated.
5. Such a system should be action oriented. It should not simply produce reports of aggregated data. It should also provide managers with information oriented toward exceptional situations which indicates the *need* to act and the *preferred* action.
6. Competition information can be gained from a variety of sources, many of which might superficially seem to be unprofitable.
7. A competition information subsystem should include a security and counterintelligence capability. This capability should rest on the assumption that competitors have a similar system and that they may resort to illegal and/or unethical means to penetrate one's own system.

Sources of information about competition

The sources of information about competitive business are numerous and diverse. One emphasis in the MMIS can be on the *organized search of publicly available information sources*. However, while much can be obtained in this fashion (e.g., by computerized and/or organized search in a business library) the information collection process at the lowest level in the organization can also be fruitful. A valuable information collector may simply be a salesperson detailed to join a plant tour at a competitor's facility and report his findings to the sales office. A clerk who has been detailed to provide a clipping service in connection with a newspaper located in a competitor's community is also performing a vital information collection function.

Much of the basic information used by marketing planners can come to them routinely from the vast outpourings of the business world's public information media—business magazines, newspapers, government publications, scholarly or scientific treatises, and continuing informal feedback from the sales force. The gaps that are not filled by these sources require that more formal collection devices be adopted.

The following is a rough guide to the collection of competition information which serves also to emphasize the diversity of sources of such information.

Field sales force. Salespeople, because of their frequent contact with customers and each other, are one of the best sources of information about competitors.

However, a salesperson is often subjected to half-truths and misleading information, particularly in the area of pricing. Information gathered by salespeople should, therefore, be cross-checked and verified by data from other sources.

Purchasing department. Supplier salespeople frequently know a great deal about what is happening in an industry. Plant tours are often available to purchasing personnel. One may take advantage of this opportunity by briefing purchasing people on what to look for.

R & D Organization. Research and development people keep up with the technical developments and breakthroughs in their various fields of interest. Their activities in technical associations and attention to technical papers and journals often give them considerable insight into competitors' product activities.

Treasury department. This information source can be valuable. If the competitor is also a customer, the treasury department will have knowledge of their payment habits and financial condition. Also, the treasury department can often arrange for introduction to key people in the financial community who have in-depth knowledge of competitor's finances.

Key executives. Key executives are often in contact with peers in the industry. These contacts can give insight into what a competitor is doing.

Business periodicals. Business periodicals are a "must." For careful scrutiny of articles dealing with a competitor's operation, the following periodicals are particularly valuable:

Wall Street Journal

Fortune

Business Week

Industrial Marketing

Printer's Ink

Harvard Business Review [9]

Business Horizons

Commerce & Business Daily

Dun's Review

---

[9] For instance, a competitor should be interested in the article by William C. Goggin, "How the Multi-dimensional Structure Works at Dow Corning," *Harvard Business Review,* January–February 1973, pp. 54–65.

Books. Books dealing with a company can be very revealing. See for example, *Managerial Decentralization* by Ronald G. Greenwood, D. C. Health & Company, Lexington, Massachusetts, 1974, which provides a study of the General Electric Company management philosophy.

Business reference services. Financial information is the strong point of business reference services. However, do not overlook this as a source of additional intelligence on other matters as well. Some standard business reference services are the following:

Moody's Industrial Manual [10]

Barron's

Standard & Poor's Industrial Surveys

Funk & Scott Index of Corporations and Industries

The Value Line Investment Survey

Dun & Bradstreet Million Dollar Directory

Standard Corporation Descriptions (Standard & Poor's Corporation)

Thomas Register of American Manufacturers

Dun & Bradstreet Reports

Business literature indices. A careful perusal of company-oriented articles in the following indices can provide useful information about a competitor. For example, two articles which were referenced in the *Business Periodicals Index* provide valuable insight into the strategic planning philosophy and approach of the General Electric Company. [11]

The Reader's Guide to Periodical Literature

The Business Periodicals Index

The Wall Street Journal Index

The New York Times Index

Applied Science and Technology Index

Business and Economic Index

[10] In one example of a particular company, this manual provided several pages of detailed information along the following organization: capital structure; history; business & products; sources of sales and earnings; principal plants and properties; management and organization; auditors; comparative consolidated income account; comparative consolidated balance sheet; financial and operating data (based on reports to Securities and Exchange Commission); long term debt profile; and capital stock data.

[11] See "GE's Jones Restructures His Top Team," *Business Week,* 30 June 1973; and C. H. Springer, "Strategic Management in General Electric," *Operations Research,* vol. 21, no. 6 (November–December 1973).

The London Times Index

The Bulletin of the Public Affairs Information Service

The Engineering Index

The Agricultural Index

Government sources

Government aerial maps, or other photographic maps can help in determining the size of a competitor's facility.

Securities and Exchange Commission reports such as "10K" reports contain very detailed information on foreign investments as well as domestic data.

Local courthouses can tell you whether a competitor is embarking on an expansion program. Courthouse files may well reveal building permits, plans, etc.

Patent Department reports

Federal Trade Commission hearings

Congressional hearings

Professional associations. Participation in professional associations can provide opportunity to talk unobtrusively with personnel of the competition.

License agreements. Some competitors are also licensees. This may help in determining something about a competitor's volume and technology.

Customers. Present and potential customers are usually interested in comparing a vendor's capabilities with those of competition. This information source is well worth developing.

Suppliers. The supplier who sells to competition has a great deal of valuable information to offer. The cooperation of the purchasing department may effectively tap this source.

Distributors. This is an outstanding source of intelligence. Distributors are often familiar with a great many aspects of a competitor's businesses.

Trade associations. Participation can yield valuable new information. The key is to gain useful intelligence without divulging very much about one's own operation.

Local chamber of commerce. This source can often give information on employment, the size of the competitor's facility and the products being manufactured at a particular location.

Local press. Many times it is worthwhile to subscribe to the local newspaper of the community where a competitor is located. The smaller the community, the more information one might find on employment, organization, expansions, etc.

Trade press. A great deal of information is published here. It is almost mandatory to review this material regularly. Sources of information concerning trade associations may be found in such publications as:

> *Directory of National Associations of Businessmen*
> *Encyclopedia of Associations*
> *Standard Advertising Register*

Stockbrokers. Particularly those who have participated in the selling of a competitor's stock, often have made in-depth studies on a competitor's strengths and weaknesses.

Annual reports. Depending somewhat on a competitor's diversity of operation, the annual report will reveal profitability and financial health as well as the names of the officers and directors. Often, there will be information regarding expansion and acquisition programs.

Prospectus. These will usually reveal the major stockholders along with financial and organizational details.

Stockholder meetings. These can be very revealing or completely unrewarding. Owners of a share of stock are entitled to ask some very pointed questions.

Local banks. A competitor's principal bank is intimately familiar with his financial position.

Investment bankers. They may be able to provide useful information. However, conflict of interest may present a problem.

Other miscellaneous sources

> Technical journals (Often, the first printed information about a new product or technology will be found here.)

Competitor's house organ

Competitor's phone directory

Competitor's former employee

Published antitrust data

Gossip from customers

Trade-show literature

Gossip by one competitor about another

Articles, papers presented at professional societies

Gossip from supplier salespeople about competitors

Information from dealers and distributors

Biographical listings (e.g., *Who's Who in America*)

Ethical Considerations

Because of the wide variety of predominantly public and semipublic information about competitors, coupled with the fact that any good information system will operate with company personnel in positions visible to other organizations, unethical or illegal methods using "secret agents" to collect competitive business information is not likely to be necessary for attaining an effective level of information. A recent survey emphasizes the current ethical approach to gathering information about competition.[12] The data collected in this study ". . . contradict an expressed belief by the respondents that ethical standards have declined." [13] This supposition is supported in other literature of the field.[14]

The use of unethical means can be counterproductive in the long run. If one pays an agent or bribes a competitor's agent to gain information, that person can undoubtedly be "bought" by the competitor, thus making the information potentially detrimental rather than beneficial. If one then uses a counterintelligence system to preclude such erroneous data, the costs of data collection will rapidly escalate to the point of negating the benefit of the original system. This argument does not even take into account the risk of exposure and resultant loss of customer goodwill and possible fines or even imprisonment. Thus, illegal and unethical activities simply do not pay in the long run.

[12] See Jerry L. Wall, "What the Competition Is Doing: You Need to Know," *Harvard Business Review,* November–December 1974.

[13] Ibid., p. 22.

[14] For instance, *Industrial Management*, "Guide to Gathering Market Intelligence," vol. 47 (March 1962), p. 84 says that ". . . the sources are so numerous . . . one need not stoop to any unethical practices. . . ."

Evaluation

The evaluation and use of competitive information is an important element of marketing planning. For instance, one company recently developed competition profiles of the people who held various positions in the competitors' organizations as well as those recently promoted and reassigned. The names of those people who had recently come into prominence in each competitive firm were then input into a commercial information system to determine the publications which each had authored.[15] A thorough study of the publication lists in one firm showed that those coming into prominence had a distinct technical bias, since they were largely technically trained people who had been contributors to a specific technical field. The inference was drawn that this technical approach would be reflected in future products of this competitor, and a strategy was developed to effectively counter new competitive products which might have these technical features.

The evaluation of competition is, in a sense, a mirror image of the strengths and weaknesses of the organization itself. The competitor's ability to conceive and to design have to be evaluated. This evaluation should concentrate on the products and design of competitors as well as on their ability to innovate in the creation, production, and marketing of their products. Evaluation of a competitor's resources must be done in a fashion which emphasizes what each can reasonably be expected to accomplish rather than solely on the resources that are available.

Competition information retrieval subsystems

Of course, highly automated retrieval systems may be developed to facilitate competitive analysis. For instance, one company has a system which provides managers with access to a data base of document abstracts. These abstracts describe articles which have appeared in more than 500 public sources—technical journals, business publications press releases, securities and exchange commission filings, and newspapers—concerning competitors.

The data base now contains over 10,000 abstracts which have been developed by a staff who scan these publications and other documents. The staff people write a brief abstract of each article and index the article in terms of (1) the competitive company to which it relates, (2) the relevant product line(s), and (3) the topical content of the article. Each of the descriptors in the three categories is chosen from a list of those with which the system is capable of dealing. For instance, the topical content list contains descriptors such as "patent," "legal," "financial," and "mergers and acquisitions."

---

[15] Such systems are currently operated on a commercial basis by both Lockheed and Systems Development Corporation.

Users of the system may inquire in terms of any of the indexing categories. One might, for example, specify a particular competitive company, or a specific product line, or a topic area. The system responds to each inquiry with an indication of the number of abstracts in the data base to give the user some idea of the magnitude of the search on which he is embarking.

Normally, a user successively specifies more than one index category. A typical inquiry is depicted in Table 5-3. There, the user begins using the system by specifying the "Competitive Abstract" data base. The system responds by indicating when the data base has most recently been updated and asking the user to enter a descriptor. In this case he first enters a competitive company name, although he could have used either a topic descriptor or a product line descriptor.

The system responds by identifying the number of articles in the data base which are indexed as relating to this company and asks for another descriptor. In this case the user then enters a product line. In effect, he has said that he wishes to know only about XYZ's widget line at this point. Again he is given the number of articles in this dual category and the system asks him to enter another descriptor. Instead, he types in "PRINT," indicating that he does not wish to further delineate the category, but instead desires a listing. The system then begins to list each of the 36 article abstracts relating to XYZ's widget line.

A retrieval system such as this is much like those which some libraries use to retrieve "information about information"—ie., to retrieve secondary information concerning the source of primary information. In this case the primary infor-

---

TABLE 5-3 Illustration of Print-out of Competition Retrieval System

DATA BASE NAME: COMPETITIVE ABSTRACT
DATA BASE UPDATED: JUNE 21, 1977
ENTER DESCRIPTOR: XYZ COMPANY
482 ARTICLES OUT OF 10,236
ENTER ANOTHER DESCRIPTOR: WIDGETS
36 ARTICLES OUT OF 482
ENTER ANOTHER DESCRIPTOR: PRINT

ARTICLE 4237
SOURCE: BUSINESS WEEK, 6,20,77, P 48
XYZ COMPANY ANNOUNCED PURCHASE OF WIDGET COMPANY OF AMERICA IN DEAL THAT HAD BEEN RUMORED FOR MONTHS. XYZ PAID 20 PERCENT ABOVE MARKET PRICE FOR 80 PERCENT OF OUTSTANDING SHARES. MARKET PRICE OF WCA STOCK HAD PREVIOUSLY DOUBLED THIS YEAR. FINANCIAL ANALYSTS QUESTION PRICE PAID. RUMORS OF QUICK EXPANSION PLANNED FOR WCA HAVE CIRCULATED SINCE PURCHASE.

ARTICLE 6023
.
.
.

---

mation is also conveyed in abstract form, but if the user desires to have the primary information—in this case the *Business Week* issue in which article 4237 appeared—he must go to the company library where it is filed by the article number.

Competitive-issue information subsystems

Another variety of subsystem which has been developed to fulfill competitive analysis needs is one that is issue oriented. Such a system is best understood by contrasting it with a pure information retrieval system. The system discussed previously retrieves secondary information—ie., information about other information. A pure retrieval system retrieves primary information directly. Pure retrieval systems require the user to specify exactly which items of information he desires from a data base of information about competitors' sales, profits, finances and so forth. The user must know in advance exactly what he wants and he must understand the way in which it is stored in the data base. Most important managerial needs for information are not so clean cut; thus, such systems seldom measure up in terms of providing critical competitive information.

A "competitive issue" competitive information system has a data base which is structured in terms of *strategic business issues*. This permits inquiries to be made in terms of *the use to which data are to be put, rather than in terms of the data themselves*. Thus, a manager using such a system inquires with a question such as, "What is the capability of Competitor X to introduce a new product in his Line Y next year?" and is presented with system responses which successively identify subclasses of data in which he may be interested. For instance, such a query might produce a system response that would identify Competitor X's financial capability, production capability, marketing capability and technological capability, as elements of the overall issue.

The user can then identify specific areas of interest, or he could indicate that he desires the total picture related to his initial question. A user indication of interest in marketing capability would produce a system response indicating the availability of data on competitive distribution channel capacity, field sales capability, service capability, technical sales experience and a variety of other marketing-related areas. The system would also indicate its ability to provide projections of future market growth. Indications of interest in other areas would produce similar system responses which would, after each new user response, indicate successively more detailed sets of available data.

Of course, such a system is limited to strategic issues and questions which have been preprogrammed. However, if the system is designed on the basis of those strategic issues and questions which are identified by user-managers to be those that are most urgently needed in supporting their decisions, it is likely to be more useful, and more used, than a pure retrieval system.

Regulatory Subsystem

Every organization operates in an environment that imposes formal constraints on it and its activities. The most obvious such constraints are government regulations. Moreover, every organization has individuals who are knowledgeable about the existing regulatory environment. However, their knowledge is often used only in an informal way, and usually after commitments have already been made in ignorance of the constraints.

The basic nature of marketing planning choices, which often involves *new* and unfamiliar areas for an organization, normally mitigates against such regulatory information being readily available to those who are doing the planning. Managers may know the regulatory environment for the products and markets that they are used to dealing with, but they cannot be expected to be familiar with the regulations surrounding *new* areas. Thus, the marketing management environment is fraught with the danger of expending planning and development resources in ignorance of crucial regulatory constraints. Such a situation cries out for a formalized data base with easy access by the many managers who participate in decision making.

The basic characteristic of a regulatory information subsystem is the same as that of any information retrieval system. The development of such a system requires that a taxonomy of the regulatory environment be developed. Then, key descriptors can be used by managers to access specific domains of the taxonomy. In this way, the regulations that are relevant to a particular product, industry, or political subdivision can be furnished to planners who have need for comprehensive regulatory information as it applies to a specific area for which choices are being made.

While there are clearly no general truths concerning the desirability and feasibility of such a subsystem, it has generally played a less important role in the minds of marketing executives than the other subsystems discussed here. Perhaps this is because it deals with boundaries rather than opportunities, and thus constrains action rather than promoting it. Or perhaps the particular design requirements of such a system, roughly analogous to that of developing a useful library indexing system, present a major cost deterrent. In any event, while such systems are technically feasible, they are generally considered only by those firms that already have been "burned" in the regulatory inferno. The current pervasiveness of such conflicts suggests that greater importance will be placed on them in the future.[16]

---

[16] For a discussion of the growing importance placed on regulatory information in business, see, for example, Liam Fahey, "Environmental Scanning: Its Conceptualization and Implementation in Twelve Large Corporations," University of Pittsburgh, Graduate School of Business, Working Paper 167 (1976).

Forecasting Subsystem

The incorporation of a forecasting subsystem into an MMIS means that the system is to operate, at least in part, so that some of the predictions (forecasts) required for any significant decision situation be provided by the system itself (i.e., in the mode of situation 4 in Figure 4-3).

Objective forecasting models

Various objective quantitative forecasting models may readily be incorporated into an MMIS. For instance, time-series forecast models seek to extrapolate historical data into the future on the basis of perceived trends, seasonal and cyclical patterns in the historical data. Other models, such as regression models, seek to predict one variable, say sales, in terms of other observable quantities, say income levels, population, and other demographics.

A third variety of quantitative forecasting model is that which can readily be developed on the basis of the customer information subsystem described earlier. Another look at Figure 5-1 will show that customer profiles can readily be used to develop sales forecasts. This is, in fact, routinely done by many firms, particularly those which market industrial products.

These various objective quantitative forecasting techniques are treated extensively in texts on business and marketing forecasting and require no elaboration here except the indication that they represent the most common variety of decision-oriented models which are incorporated into an MMIS.[17]

Subjective forecasting

However valuable forecasts of quantitatively defined variables may be, more subjective entities are also of great value to marketers. Figure 5-2 shows a value forecast made by General Electric which compares a value profile for the year 1969 with the forecasted profile for 1980.[18] The profiles are not depicted on a quantitative scale; rather they reflect points on a scale between contrasting value pairs. While such a forecast is imprecise, it illustrates the value shifts which are expected to occur in the 1969–1980 period.

Delphi forecasting

The Delphi forecasting approach was developed as a method of eliciting expert opinion about the future in a systematic fashion. Such opinion forecasts are fa-

[17] For instance, see S. C. Wheelwright and S. Makridakis, *Forecasting Methods for Management* (New York: Wiley, 1973) and C. W. Gross and R. T. Peterson, *Business Forecasts* (New York: Houghton Mifflin, 1976).

[18] Reprinted with permission of Ian H. Wilson and the General Electric Company.

miliar and valuable inputs to marketing. For instance, McGraw-Hill's surveys of business people's plans for making expenditures on plant and equipment are published regularly in *Business Week* and are widely used as forecasting bases. Other forecasts are made by obtaining the collective judgment of groups. However, forecasts based on composites of group opinion have often been found to represent *compromises* rather than *consensuses* since such things as the prestige or

FIGURE 5-2 Profile of significant value system changes

1969–1980 as seen by General Electric's Business Environment section

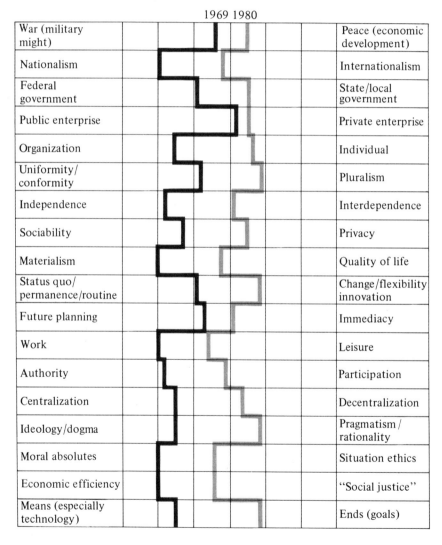

1969 1980		
War (military might)		Peace (economic development)
Nationalism		Internationalism
Federal government		State/local government
Public enterprise		Private enterprise
Organization		Individual
Uniformity/conformity		Pluralism
Independence		Interdependence
Sociability		Privacy
Materialism		Quality of life
Status quo/permanence/routine		Change/flexibility innovation
Future planning		Immediacy
Work		Leisure
Authority		Participation
Centralization		Decentralization
Ideology/dogma		Pragmatism/rationality
Moral absolutes		Situation ethics
Economic efficiency		"Social justice"
Means (especially technology)		Ends (goals)

▬▬▬▬ 1969 Values Profile   ▬▬▬▬ 1980 Values Profile

personality of individuals can inordinately influence the judgment of a group.

Delphi is a technique which enables a group of experts to contribute to one another's understanding and to refine their opinions as a result of interaction with other experts.[19] Delphi physically separates the experts, however, so that individuals and their rationales do not become submerged in the overt activities of a group. The steps involved in the Delphi process are (1) predictions by each expert, (2) clarification by a neutral investigator, (3) requestioning of experts combined with feedback from other experts.

The process of requestioning is designed to eliminate misinterpretation and to bring to the attention of each expert elements of knowledge which may not be known to all.

Modifications to the basic Delphi are too numerous to detail. However, almost all modified Delphis are designed to achieve authentic consensus and valid results by (1) anonymity of respondents, (2) statistical response, and (3) iterative polling with feedback.

Turoff has identified a number of aims of Delphi which suggest its potential utility: [20]

> . . . to determine or develop a range of possible alternatives
>
> . . . to explore underlying assumptions or information leading to differing assumptions
>
> . . . to correlate informed judgments on topics spanning a wide range of disciplines
>
> . . . to educate respondents as to the diverse and interrelated aspects of a topic
>
> . . . to generate consensus

Delphi, of course, is not without its detractors.[21] However, it is obviously a variety of judgmental model which is readily systematized, and many companies use Delphi in one form or another on a routine basis. In its MMIS context, Delphi forecasting may be used to address social trends and the nature and timing of their impact on products and markets. Such forecasts are the essential informational underpinnings of new-product decisions and marketing strategy.

Computer programs have been developed for performing the calculations and providing the output of each round in a useful and standardized format to those who are participating. Thus, Delphi forecasts, as well as other varieties of subjective forecasts, are readily incorporable into a sophisticated MMIS.

---

[19] For reports on Delphi and derivations of it used by TRW, Inc., see "New Products: Setting a Timetable," *Business Week,* 27 May, 1967, pp. 52–56.

[20] M. Turoff, "The Design of a Policy Delphi," *Technological Forecasting and Social Change,* vol. 2 (1970), pp. 149–171.

[21] See H. Sackman, *Delphi Critique* (Lexington, Mass.: Lexington Books, 1975), and N. C. Dalkey, *Studies on the Quality of Life: Delphi and Decision Making* (Lexington, Mass.: Lexington Books, 1972), as well as basic texts such as J. P. Martino, *Technological Forecasting for Decision Making* (New York: Elsevier, 1972).

Cost-Benefit Subsystem

The cost-benefit subsystem is that MMIS subsystem which supports decision making. In many situations, marketing decisions will be made on the basis of the *informed* subjective judgment of the manager, based on information provided to him by the other MMIS subsystems. However, it may be beneficial that his decision making be supported by formalized decision models. (In other words, the overall MMIS may, for some decisions, operate in the mode of situation 3 or 4 in Figure 4-3 rather than in situation 2 in that figure.)

The cost-benefit subsystem is, therefore, decision-model oriented, and it has the objective of assessing the worth of contemplated actions or strategies. This worth is assessed in terms of things to be gained (benefits) and resources to be consumed (costs). In business, the net measure of *profit*, which is benefits (revenues) minus cost, is usually the overall measure which is to be assessed, but the benefit/cost analysis need not be so narrow. For instance, many firms today also try to assess the social benefits and costs which may result from their actions despite the fact that these social consequences may not directly affect profitability. They do this because of their concern with society's betterment and because of the potential long-range negative consequences to them if they create products and take actions which are detrimental to society as a whole (e.g., from further government regulation or from legal proceedings which may be entered against them for such things as unsafe products).

The cost-benefit subsystem may be of many varieties. Here, we illustrate cost-benefit models in terms of a simulation model which is, among other things, designed to answer "what if?" questions concerning proposed actions. The answers to these questions are given in cost-benefit terms.

Figure 5-3 shows the conceptual outline of such a simulation model as developed for a business firm. The profit model module is the calculational core of the overall model. It takes the interrelated outputs from four varieties of models and projects the volume, profit, and profitability consequences for various sets of conditions. The four general inputs to the profit model are from:

1. Market-oriented models
   a. Sales-service model
   b. Market model
   c. Competitive model
2. Marketing cost model
3. Product cost model
4. Environmental model

The first of the three market-oriented submodels depicts sales and service relationships in the business in question. The business involves the sale of capital

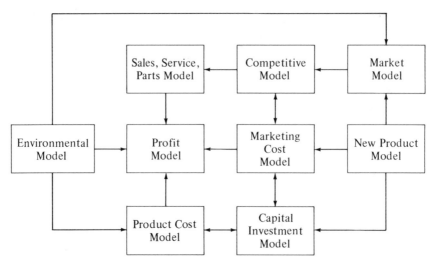

FIGURE 5-3 Business decision model

equipment and the subsequent sale of parts, service, and service contracts. This model utilizes historical patterns to project the distribution of future service and maintenance revenues to be anticipated because of current sales of capital equipment. It also uses inputs from the market and competitive models to project future service revenues to be expected on competitive equipment based on competitor's sales projections.

The other two market-oriented submodels are the market and competitive models. The market submodel projects the market for this variety of equipment based on data on construction activity patterns in a variety of geographic areas and construction types. The competitive model uses past and projected competitive practices and patterns in the industry to predict how the total market will be divided among the competitors.

The profit model also processes the outputs of marketing and product cost models, which project these cost elements under various conditions, and an environmental model, which primarily involves inflationary and other uncontrollable economic forces.

The other submodels in Figure 5-3, capital investment and new products, are used to analyze specific strategies involving either or both of these elements (e.g., a process investment intended to reduce production cost or a new product). The outputs of these models are fed into the overall profit model through other submodels as shown by the arrows in the figure.

The uses of such corporate models are manifold. The particular model of Figure 5-3 was used for three general purposes:

1. Testing proposed strategies through the posing of "what if?" questions
2. Analysis of the sensitivity of overall business performance to changes in various factors
3. Forecasting business performance

As an illustration of these uses, consider the three questions below, each of which is an actual request by management for a model run—one for each of the above categories.

1. What would happen if we went out of the X segment of our business over the next two years and began producing for the Y market as soon as possible?
2. How important is the combined effect of (a) our improved warranty and (b) the anticipated improvement in our capacity to generate sales in parts and services?
3. Suppose that we forecast the following changes in construction over the next few years, what would be the effect?
   Family dwellings down 10 percent per year
   Apartments up 15 percent next year and 10 percent per year thereafter
   Government building down 5 percent per year

The model represented in Figure 5-3 presented answers for each of these questions in terms of financial projections of revenues, income, and ROI (return on investment) on a year-by-year basis in both actual dollars and present dollars (corrected for inflation). These projections are made for various business lines.

When the projected consequences of any question such as those above are compared with a base case, that is, a projection which has been agreed to represent a surprise-free projection or a business-as-usual scenario, the potential value of such a model becomes clear. For instance, "what if?" strategy questions serve to evaluate proposed strategies directly. Even if one is unwilling to use the model as the final basis for choice, such projections often serve to delineate poor strategies (thus saving further evaluative effort) and to highlight potentially good strategies for further analysis.

Sensitivity questions of the variety of question 2 above serve to define what is important and what is relatively less important. This, although seemingly simple, is, in fact, one of the primary values of such models, because analyses conducted in other ways cannot so readily isolate single factors, pairs of factors, etc., in terms of their relative importance. For instance, in the company involved in the model of Figure 5-3, a study group presented a report to top management which resulted in a morning-long discussion concerning various strategy elements—production cost improvements, material utilization and the potential sale of a production facility. At lunch, the chief executive said, "Let's see what the model says about this!'' Various runs of the model were made over the lunch break, with the result that all three strategy elements, having consumed the entire morning's discussion, were shown to have relatively little strategic impact on the firm's long-run future!

Simulation models can also be used in forecasting, as illustrated by the third question above. In the company in question, this use of the model provided insights which resulted in a regional strategy for the company's marketing effort. Such a strategy had never been contemplated until the differential construction activity forecasts for various construction segments in various parts of the country, coupled with a marketing and distribution cost analysis, showed that a uniform nationwide strategy would be clearly inferior to one which emphasized different products in various geographical areas.

Intelligence Subsystem

As used here, the term *intelligence* refers to specific facts or the answers to specific questions concerning happenings in the environment. For instance, the answer to a question concerning a competitor's intentions to bid or not bid on a project is an intelligence item, as is an assessment that a potential customer will soon be changing suppliers.

The usual definition of the term is broader than that used here. For instance, the competitor profiles and other aspects of the various information systems previously discussed also qualify under the more widely accepted military use of the term. Here, however, they are incorporated into other subsystems and specifically excluded from the intelligence subsystem (which focuses on obtaining answers to specific questions about the competitor rather than on the maintenance of continually updated profiles of competitors and customers).

The critical aspects of intelligence gathering are *organization* and *systemization*. It is not the purpose here to enumerate the myriad data sources and data collection requirements for a good intelligence system,[22] but rather to establish the desirability of having a formalized intelligence system and the authority and responsibility patterns that are appropriate for effective intelligence activities.

The critical point in the intelligence subsystem, as in the potential customer and competition information subsystems, is to gather intelligence information systematically, to have it evaluated, aggregated, and analyzed by trained people, and to ensure that it is distributed to those decision makers who can make use of it. If this can be done in a parsimonious fashion so that the great amount of redundant and irrelevant information already flowing around in the organization

[22] See, for example, David I. Cleland and William R. King, *Management: A Systems Approach* (New York: McGraw-Hill, 1972), chap. 17.

is not merely made larger, the benefits can far outweigh the costs of such an operation.

In the development of a marketing intelligence system, the most important element is the people who will develop and implement it. Moreover, the most important factor in determining its effectiveness is the recognition that *everyone* in an organization is involved both in the marketing function and in the process of intelligence gathering. The engineer who discusses specifications with the customer is both a marketer and an intelligence agent, as is the field marketing representative. Indeed, technical people can often have marketing impact of a far different and more significant variety than can the professional marketer or undercover agent. So, too, is top management involved both in marketing and in the collection of market intelligence. One of the most significant results of the image survey example described earlier was the recognition by the company that their top management, who had preached a customer-oriented marketing approach for years, were not themselves personally customer oriented.

An effective approach to ensure that nonmarketers play their marketing intelligence roles is to specifically integrate them into the intelligence gathering network. When engineers are to have customer contact, they must be made aware of what critical information is needed and who in the customer's organization is likely to have it. Top management should be similarly briefed before their visits to customers and debriefed on return. In this way, a great deal of relevant information can be garnered and provided to those decision makers who are in need of it.

Of course, all this presumes that an office in the organization has been set up for the collection and analysis of intelligence information. The analysis of intelligence involves a determination of the relevance, credibility, value, and appropriate dissemination of intelligence data. This central office can also perform the function of gathering together the key questions and identifying the voids in the knowledge necessary for effective strategic marketing planning. These questions can be asked in a routine fashion of field personnel and others who might be expected to have relevant information. Often, these people have the desired information in one form or another; but without a formalized intelligence system they have no way of getting it to the right people or of having it integrated with other information to form useful information aggregates.

This same intelligence organization—with its focus on analysis, eliminating redundancies, posing questions, and disseminating information to those who are in need of it—can also function as a part of the competitive and potential customer information subsystems. For example, data provided by clipping services require much the same analysis whether they relate to competitors or customers.

Of course, any system which is oriented toward the collection of specific facts or items of information in response to the inquiries of its user-managers will usually be highly "labor intensive." This is so because data which are collected are not intelligence until they have been analyzed and interpreted by the substantive experts. In cases of urgency, information can be passed to the decision makers without scrutiny by the substantive experts; but when time permits (and this means in the great majority of the cases), it is processed, finished intelligence that is of greatest use by the decision maker.

The quality of the analysis and interpretation depends to a large degree on the credentials the analyst holds. In the business organization, that means that the one having functional responsibility (production, marketing, finance, or R & D) is the best one to interpret a particular "functional" type of information. Determining the probable strategy of a competitor in the penetration of a new market area could be handled by a mix of people from several functional areas of the organization. The "war gaming" of a competitor's strategy would best be handled by setting up a microcompany within the organization to study the data that have intelligence value, and then hypothesizing what the competitor's strategy might be.

In any case, there is the need for a centralized processing unit—in many cases of "start up" situations, perhaps only a single person. For instance, one company set up an individual who began by sending out a "want list" containing questions that needed to be answered concerning competitive actions on certain key company programs. This list was updated weekly. The field salesmen and others who received this list were urged to communicate anything that might be of significance about competitors to the intelligence office. Through this simple device, much was learned about competitive technical and marketing strategy— particularly concerning a major government project on which the company was preparing a proposal.

The dissemination of intelligence is the process of distributing the finished intelligence to those persons and agencies entitled to receive it. If the nature of the intelligence relates to strategic planning, then the people who prepare plans and are responsible for making strategic decisions should be the recipients of the finished intelligence. Certain information, sensitive in nature, may be distributed to only select individuals. Within the military establishment, the concept of "needing to know" prevails; that is, regardless of an individual's organizational position, a person should receive only intelligence that is necessary in order for him to carry out his managerial duties. The same general idea can be carried to a business organization.

However labor intensive such systems are, they may be computerized. For instance, one firm collects, in standard format, all intelligence reports from its field salespeople and visitors to other cities. It keeps these reports in computer memory where they can be accessed in a variety of ways—by name of competitor, name of product, date, etc. Table 5-4 shows a (censored) version of a portion of a printout from this system. This run was initiated by inquiries using the name of a competitor.

TABLE 5-4 Sample of an Intelligence Print-Out

DATE	REPORTER ORIGIN PRODUCTS	AGENCY	ABSTRACT
23 OCTOBER 1975	F. S. SMITH MD V	CO206-XYZ CORP Q DIVISION BALTIMORE, MD	THE FOLLOWING OBTAINED FROM AN ARTICLE IN LOCAL PRESS (1) HEAD OF DIVISION IS G. H. JONES (2) H. B. SMITH IN CHARGE OF TEST (3) SYS AT JONES AIRPORT COST ABOUT $4.5M (4) PRODUCT WEIGHS 12k LBS EMPTY
25 OCTOBER 1975	P. R. JOHNSON PGH W	CO183 SH&F CO. CONSULTANTS BALTIMORE, MD CO206 XYZ CORP Q DIVISION BALTIMORE, MD	SH&F IS A CORP. OF PLANNERS, ARCHITECTS, AND ENGINEERS DEALING WITH XYZ TYPE BUSINESS. THEY APPEAR TO BE WELL STRUCTURED AND EMPLOY 150–200 PEOPLE, TWO COMPUTERS, COMMAND GOOD FEES, AND HANDLE CONTRACT IN 200–300k RANGE. THEY ARE WORKING WITH XYZ ON TWO PROJECTS AT A AND B. XYZ ENGINEERS ARE PLANT ORIENTED AND INEXPERIENCED IN POLITICAL ENVIRONMENT OF THIS FIELD.
29 OCTOBER 1975	J. E. MULLINS WSH V	CO111 ABD CO. CONSULTANTS WASHINGTON, D.C. CO206 XYZ CORP Q DIVISION BALTIMORE, MD	WALTER OF ABD HAS BEEN CALLING ON XYZ FOR 10 YEARS. SAYS THEY ARE DISCONTINUING NEGOTIATIONS ON A PROJECT AND THAT ALL WORK HAS STOPPED IN DISPUTE ON PROJECT B.

113

Summary

MMIS subsystems can be created in many different ways to suit the business and needs of a particular organization. This chapter identified and described some MMIS subsystems which should prove to be widely useful to business firms who wish to develop an MMIS.

The internal operations subsystem is that which already exists to process transactions and provide operational control information in the organization. It is the base on which the more analytically oriented subsystems can be built.

The customer information subsystem serves to develop aggregate customer information, trend information, and customer profiles to support factual decision making about sales promotion as well as longer-run decisions concerning products and markets.

Image information subsystems address subjective perceptions about the organization as it exists in the minds of important clientele such as customers. Such a subsystem serves to complement the objective information provided by the customer information subsystem.

The potential-customer information subsystem deals with those market segments or individual consuming units who have not been customers, but who have needs that are related to those of current customers.

The goals and policies subsystem aggregates organizational goals and policies into a form and place which is accessible and usable by managers.

The competition and intelligence subsystems compile information about competitors so that it can be used as a basis for developing competitive marketing strategy. The two subsystems are closely related; however, the former includes the development and updating of competition profiles, while the latter focuses on the answering of specific questions relative to competitors' actions.

The regulatory subsystem contains information on laws, rulings of regulatory agencies, and other legal constraints which might inhibit marketing strategy.

The forecasting and cost-benefit subsystems focus on the use of models to develop predictions, recommended actions, and the answers to "what if?" questions about the consequences of proposed actions.

All these subsystems taken together form the overall MMIS. However, an organization does not need to have all of them in order to have an effective MMIS. The specialized systems should be developed in accordance with their relative importance to the overall business and the degree to which the subsystem outputs can effectively integrated into marketing decision making.

EXERCISES

1. Which of the following items of information would normally be routinely provided by the operational level MMIS?
   a. Price for an order
   b. Quantity purchased on an order
   c. Customer name for an order
   d. Customer location for an order
   e. Sales by product
   f. Sales by salesman
   g. Profitability by product

2. How can aggregate customer information, as depicted in Table 5-1, be used to determine the following?
   a. Optimum frequency of sales calls
   b. Optimum number of salesmen
   c. Optimum compensation plan for salespeople

3. Take the verbal answer which you have given in question 2 and try to develop a simple algebraic model which expresses in mathematical terms the relationships you expressed. Do this by using a symbol to represent the measures at the head of each column in Table 5-1.

4. How might trend information related to the quantities in Table 5-1 change your answers to questions 2 and 3?

5. In Figure 5-1, suppose that the industry trend for next year was 10 percent and that all factors not affected by that trend remain the same. What sales objective might be established?

6. Suppose that the industry factors in Figure 5-1 are not available. How could a sales objective be set in the face of this lack of information?

7. Give an illustration of how the lack of a goals and policy subsystem might lead to inconsistent choices on the part of middle-level marketing managers.

8. Put yourself in the position of an employee who is offered a large cash payment in return for some critical marketing information on your employer's products. Suppose that you do it and get away with it. What is likely to happen the next time that your "customer" wants information?

9. Suppose you are a manager and it has been suggested to you that an offer of a job should be made to a competitor's employee primarily because he is believed to know some critical information about your competitor. What factors would you consider in making such a decision?

10. What difficulties can you foresee in designing and operating a regulatory information subsystem?

11. What marketing uses of Delphi can you think of for the following?
    a. To determine or develop a range of possible alternatives
    b. To explore underlying assumptions or information leading to differing assumptions

c. To correlate informed judgments on topics spanning a wide range of disciplines

d. To educate respondents as to the diverse and interrelated aspects of a topic

12. What role do you think possible "social impact" should play in analyzing alternative marketing decisions? Give some examples of *measures* of social impact which might be incorporated into the data base of an MMIS.

13. Why is it desirable to compare simulation model projections which reflect different circumstances to a base-case surprise-free projection?

14. Discuss the important value of "academic" sensitivity analyses, using models such as that of Figure 5-2, in the context of the following statement made by a business executive: "The single greatest failure in strategic marketing planning is that of identifying the highest impact strategies."

15. What is the difference between the intelligence subsystem and the competition subsystem as outlined in Chapter 5? Why do you suppose this distinction has been made?

REFERENCES

Barclay, Stephen. *The Secrets Business.* New York: Crowell, 1973.

Business Week, August 4, 1975. "Business Sharpens Its Spying Techniques."

Chemical Engineering, April 25, 1966. "Gathering Competitive Information."

DeCarbonnel, F. E., and Dorrance, Roy G. "Information Sources for Planning Decisions." *California Management Review* XV (Summer 1973):42–53.

Greene, Richard M., ed. *Business Intelligence and Espionage.* Homewood, Ill: Irwin, 1966.

Hamilton, Peter. *Espionage and Subversion in an Industrial Society.* London: Hutchinson, 1967.

Hodge, B. "The Computer in Management Information and Control Systems." *Data Management,* December 1974, pp. 26–30.

Kelley, W. T. "Marketing Intelligence for Top Management." *Journal of Marketing,* October 1965.

Kotler, P. "A Design for the Firm's Marketing Nerve Center." *Business Horizons,* Fall 1966.

Lanahan, J. "Data Base Applications at Inland Steel." *Data Base,* Winter 1973, pp. 87–94.

Pokempner, S. J. "Management Information Systems: A Pragmatic Survey." *The Conference Board Record,* May 1973, pp. 49–54.

Thomas, Philip S. Marketing Intelligence Systems: A Dew Line for Marketing Men." *Business Management,* January 1966.

———. "Environmental Analysis for Corporate Planning." *Business Horizons,* October 1974, pp. 27–37.

Well, Jerry L. "What Competition Is Doing: Your Need to Know." *Harvard Business Review,* November–December 1974.

6

Principles and Strategies
for MMIS Design

I n this chapter, we turn from the nature of the MMIS to the process which can be used to design, develop, and implement the MMIS. The MMIS which is to serve a complex firm cannot readily be purchased and installed for the use of the firm. Rather, to be most useful, it must be developed from within; perhaps with the aid of consultants and hardware vendors, but certainly with the input and participation of the managers who will be the system's ultimate users.

The process of designing and developing an MMIS is not a definitive one. Just as the MMIS must be designed to suit the unique needs of the organization, so too must the design process be so suited. There exists no correct MMIS design process which can be provided to the reader.

Indeed, the title of this chapter suggests that there are certain principles of MMIS design which can be universally applied. Of course, even this is not really true. There are no universally valid design principles.

The best available foundation for an MMIS design and development process is a set of principles which reflect the best that is known about factors which have led to the design of good, useful systems, as well as how factors which have led to system design failures may be avoided. These principles are neither universally valid nor eternally valid. One or more may not be applicable to any given organization and one or more may be shown to be invalid or improved upon on the basis of future experience.

However, the principles are valid bases for *beginning* the process of designing the design process in any organization. And, if the design process to be used is one which does not adhere to one or more of these principles, a strong justification for such a deviation should be developed. In effect then, the design principles expounded here are *standards* by which the design process which a particular firm develops may be assessed.

In most cases, design principles can be implemented through *design strategies*—broad "how to do it" statements of direction for the MMIS development effort. Such strategies are generally described in this chapter; operationalizing is discussed in subsequent chapters.

The Importance of Relevant Information

The caricature of the harried manager sitting amidst stacks of computer printouts while longing for a crucial item of information that can aid him in making a decision is a very real description of the state of organizations and their computerized information systems. The proliferation of computers and computerized data processing systems has led to the collection, processing, and consequent availability to managers of more information than they can possibly use effectively. Yet, at the same time, managers still have a need for crucial pieces of information that their systems do not possess or, alternately, that they do not know how to identify and retrieve from their complex systems.

Thus, one might well say that information systems currently provide managers with an *overabundance of data and a corresponding paucity of relevant information*. This clearly says that the MMIS should not be designed merely to provide more information; indeed, the best MMIS may very well provide the manager with less total data than he previously had. A good MMIS will, however, provide him with more *relevant* information.

The first principle of MMIS design, therefore, has to do with *parsimony:* the manager should be provided with the *minimum amount of relevant information* that he needs to perform his job effectively, and no more.

Of course, an inquiry capability may be incorporated into the system to allow for the broader needs of individuals in specific circumstances, but the basic structure of the system must have the objective of providing the most useful relevant information without inundating the manager with masses of less useful data. The inquiry capability gives the manager access to a broader range of data than that with which he is routinely supplied. This permits him to go beyond the limits of normal reports to explore. But he does this on a selective and elective basis rather than by being overburdened with masses of data that he cannot possibly use.

Exception reporting

This criterion may be implemented, in part, by exception reporting. Exception reporting is the way in which an information system can implement the management principle of *management by exception*. In layman's terms, the management by exception idea says that the manager should devote the major portion of his time and energy to the management of exceptional circumstances—those things which are operating abnormally or are out of control—rather than to managing those things which are operating smoothly.

Exception reporting is that model of system operation in which only exceptions are reported to the manager. Those elements of his concern which are operating as expected within prescribed limits go unreported unless the manager chooses to ask questions or inquire for reports.

In this mode, the MMIS itself has built-in decision rules for determining if and when exceptions have occurred. For instance, a simple exception-oriented rule might specify that salespeople's expenses be reported to the sales manager only if they deviate from the budget by more than 10 percent. Under such a rule, a sales manager might go for months without any reports on some salesperson with the full confidence that things are OK as defined by the decision rule which has been programmed into the system.

If he wishes to check up on the system or to make an assessment of sales expenses which requires a finer level of detail than that provided by the rule concerning 10 percent of the budget, he must ask for it. While this may be a little bit of trouble, the benefit which derives in return is to avoid being deluged each month with voluminous sales reports from all salespeople.

User-Based Systems

A basic criterion for developing a useful MMIS is that *the system must satisfy the perceived needs of its user-managers.* A wide variety of studies have reached this general conclusion,[1] despite the fact that there is a difference between managers' wants and their needs. This has been widely discussed in the literature of information systems.[2]

The major reason for this focus on the user is a very practical one: evidence suggests that managers will simply not use systems which are not designed from such a perspective. Illustrations are legion in the field of MIS of multimillion-dollar information systems which are not used, or else not used for the intended purpose. Usually, the primary reason for this lack of use is simply that the system does not do what the potential users thought it was supposed to do, or else that it does not do the desired things in an *acceptable* way, that is, in a way that the managers understand and feel comfortable with.

Of course, as noted in an earlier chapter, this principle does not imply that systems should be developed solely because managers have stated a need; nor should they be developed to do only what managers wish them to do, in ways that managers prescribe. If systems were slavishly designed to conform to managerial criteria, the likely result would be organizational stagnation.

A User-Oriented Systems
Optimality Criterion

The user-oriented design principle leads naturally to the development of an optimality criterion for systems design.

In most system design efforts, analysts establish the criterion to be used for

---

[1] See for example, A. Chandler, *Strategy and Structure: Chapters in the History of the Industrial Enterprise* (Cambridge, Mass.: MIT Press, 1962); John Child, "Organizational Structure, Environment and Performance: The Role of Strategic Choice," *Sociology,* vol. 6, no. 1 (January 1972), pp. 2–22; R. M. Cyert and J. G. March, *A Behavioral Theory of the Firm* (Englewood Cliffs, N.J.: Prentice-Hall, 1963); R. Normann, "Some Conclusions from 13 Case Studies of New Product Development," S.I.A.R. Report, No. UPM-RM-100, Stockholm, 1969); and K. E. Weick, *The Social Psychology of Organizing* (Reading, Mass.: Addison-Wesley, 1969).

[2] See for example, R. L. Ackoff, "Management Misinformation Systems," *Management Science,* vol. 14, no. 4 (December 1967), pp. B147–B156; William R. King and David I. Cleland, "The Design of Management Information Systems: An Information Analysis Approach," *Management Science,* November, 1975.

judging which systems design is best. Whether that criterion involves the ability of a model to produce accurate predictions, the speed and accuracy of data processing, or the degree to which the system is able to replicate actual operating history, the criterion is almost invariably technical in nature. *It does not generally involve a measure of, or even the objective consideration of, the acceptability and usefulness of the system to its prospective users.*

The validity of this claim concerning systems design criteria is made evident by most descriptions of systems design or problem solving processes.[3] Such process descriptions invariably treat implementation consideration as one of the latter stages of the design process. Moreover, the treatment of this implementation phase is generally less objective and scientific than is the treatment of the earlier design phases.

This relegation of implementation questions to the latter phases of the design process suggests that the optimal system (in the technical sense) is developed first and *then* the designer considers what he must do in order to get this design accepted and used by the user. *This afterthought view of implementation questions implicitly relegates them to a low level of relative importance and explicitly restricts the feasible range of implementation alternatives.*

An alternative criterion for system optimality goes beyond simple technical optimality to incorporate implementation considerations into every step of problem solving or systems design processes. The underlying premise of this broader concept of optimality is simple: *that it is far better to develop an improved system which is implemented, than to develop one which is theoretically optimal but which is not implemented.*

This design criterion is clearly based on a view of systems design as primarily an applied activity, since it devalues theoretically optimal designs which are not implemented. Indeed, it even goes so far as to devalue systems which were not developed and designed specifically to have a high likelihood of being implemented, even if those systems are, in fact, implemented in a particular situation.

The idea of a broader concept of optimality which incorporates implementation considerations into every stage of the design process is consistent with much of the implementation-oriented thinking which has gone on in recent years, as exemplified by Churchman and Schainblatt's [4] manager researcher "mutual understanding" and by Mason and Mitroff's [5] "principles" regarding the needs of managers for information that suits their psychology and for methods of generating evidence that is geared to their problems. It would appear to be generally

---

[3] For instance, see S. Eilon, "How Scientific is OR?" *OMEGA*, vol. 3, no. 1 (1975), pp. 1–8.

[4] C. W. Churchman and A. H. Schainblatt, "The Researcher and the Manager: A Dialectic of Implementation," *Management Science*, February 1965.

[5] R. O. Mason and I. I. Mitroff, "A Program for Research on Management Information Systems," *Management Science*, January 1973.

agreed that, except in very special circumstances, if an analyst and his client-manager do not have such mutual understanding and if the system output does not suit their psychology and needs, a good manager is unlikely to be willing to accept the decision support provided by the MMIS.

Indeed, in the field of management information systems this implementation problem has been viewed as a function of lack of understanding between managers and analyst such that a high-level committee of the Association for Computing Machinery has recommended the creation of a new MIS job position.[6] The primary function of the new position is to serve as an intermediary between manager and analyst, so that their lack of understanding of each other's roles and methodologies will not prevent the successful implementation of information systems.

Thus, the old controversy about whether better implementation is to be achieved by developing better, more analytic managers who are able to understand the sophisticated models and computer systems of the analyst, or by giving analysts training in management to ensure their understanding of the complexities of the real-world manager's job, is apparently to be resolved in the MIS field by giving up on both possibilities and interposing an individual with an entirely new variety of skills to operate between manager and analyst.

The idea treated here is not for the creation of a new position, but rather for the acceptance of a new concept of optimality in systems design—a concept which encompasses both technical optimality and the "implementability" of the system and which is applied *at every stage of systems design*. By using this design criterion, the designer will sometimes sacrifice technical performance to gain greater likelihood of acceptance of the system by its manager-users. His ideal technical design is unlikely to be the final design which results from a design process which uses this criterion. However, if such a criterion does significantly influence the acceptability of the system to managers, the criterion will have achieved the objective of all MMIS development real-world decision support.

Cost-Effective Systems Design

Another basic principle of systems design has to do with cost effectiveness. *An MMIS has the objective of decision support, but only insofar as the decision support results in gains for the organization which more than offset the system costs.*

That this obvious point needs to be stated might seem questionable to the

---

[6] See R. L. Ashenhurst (ed.), "Curriculum Recommendations for Graduate Professional Programs in Information Systems: A Report of the ACM Curriculum Committee on Computer Education for Management," *Communications of the ACM,* vol. 15, no. 5 (May 1972), pp. 363–398.

uninitiated. However, many systems have been developed to keep up with the Joneses in terms of the degree of computerization of the firm's management activities; and many systems have been designed which are so uniquely oriented toward individual managers that they are not found to be useful by other individuals when they move into the same managerial slot.

Thus, despite the user orientation for the MMIS which is suggested by the foregoing principles, such a system cannot be designed to idiosyncratically provide the specific information desired by each individual manager. To provide such a capability would require inordinate development costs and continuous basic system changes as managers changed positions and people entered and left the organization. Thus, if such a system is to be efficient, *it must provide various classes of managers with specific categories of information to support their decisions.*

Although managers' perceived needs are taken to be a valid basis for system design, these perceived needs must reflect the *collective* wisdom of some relatively homogeneous group of *experienced* managers rather than reflecting needs as perceived by any individual. This concept of collective needs for information allows for the development of an information system which provides a manager with a set of information which has been assessed to be needed by an *experienced* class of people occupying a specified position rather than by a specific individual. This obvious cost-effective approach, therefore, has the added benefit of enabling the system to educate the novice manager by providing information which he might not personally be able to identify as important, or even relevant.

This means that costly special-purpose subsystems should be evaluated carefully with regard to their contribution, particularly if those subsystems are designed to conform to the particular interests or perceived need of specific individuals in the organization.

However, the principle of cost effectiveness is perhaps most often violated at the other extreme. Cost-effectiveness criteria have become so endemic in some organizations that the primary criterion for systems design is cost savings. Thus, if a system can be demonstrated to be capable of replacing several clerks and file cabinets, it can readily be justified on these economic grounds. However, if it is the sort of system which is oriented to providing the organization with new capabilities—say, with the capability of assessing competition—it is much less easy to justify. The expectation is that such a system will be justified in terms of benefits (e.g., greater revenues and market shares) rather than in terms of cost savings, but it is harder to show such benefits in concrete terms.

The principle of cost effectiveness can therefore be violated in a variety of ways despite its apparent straightforward nature. The wise manager and analyst will be aware of all these varieties of violations and take steps to avoid them.

Manager-Analyst Cooperative Design

The preceding principles concerning both a user-oriented system and a criterion oriented toward implementation optimality suggest that *systems should be designed using a joint manager-analyst cooperative effort.*

There is ample evidence that this obvious principle is not widely applied. For instance, a McKinsey and Co. report reveals that "many otherwise effective top managements are in trouble with their computer efforts because they have abdicated control to staff specialists." [7] A computer survey also "indicates that technicians, not management, are setting goals for the computers." [8]

The deficiencies that are inherent in an analyst-oriented design process are readily apparent. Computer systems analysts generally are unaware of the myriad complexities of management decisions. They cannot know all the subjectivities and intangibles. Therefore, the systems they design do not account for subtleties and are often no more helpful to the manager than the stacks of hand-produced reports he previously had at hand. The speed with which computerized systems make data available is useful, but information systems clearly have not made for a revolution in management as many thought they would.

The reasons that managers have often abdicated their design responsibilities are also clear. A manager best knows the job of managing, not the job of systems design. Systems design and development and the intricacies of such things as operating systems and file structures are beyond his expertise. It is therefore natural for him, over the long period that is usually required for systems design and development, to retire to those things that he knows best, leaving the systems design to the analysts. This is a natural process and takes place often, even in those situations where the dangers are recognized in advance and both analysts and managers are admonished at the beginning of a design effort to make sure "it does not happen to us."

The solution to the problem is conceptually clear. Since neither the manager nor the analyst alone can design and implement a true management information system, they must work cooperatively. Each must make his own unique contribution, and anything short of complete cooperation will probably result in a systems design that is either ineffective or inefficient.

However, the practical ways in which this principle may be put into practice are not so clear as is the concept. In a later chapter, we shall devote a good portion of our systems design methodology to describing such an operational approach to implementing this principle.

[7] "Unlocking the Computer's Profit Potential," in *Computers and Automation* (New York: McKinsey and Co., Inc., April 1969).

[8] John Diebold, "Bad Decisions on Computer Use," *Harvard Business Review,* January– February 1969.

Achieving Managerial Understanding

While the cooperative design process may be the best way of achieving managerial understanding of the system and its operation, the principle is important enough to stand alone regardless of the approach taken to its fulfillment.

The principle is, simply stated, that *managers must understand the MMIS so that they will be willing to use it and so that they will be able to control it and not be controlled by it.*

The era of faith, in which management scientists and computer consultants operated by first having the manager describe his problem and then developing a model or system to cope with it, and presenting the "answer" or finished system to the manager, is fast coming to an end. Managers are no longer awed by computers and models; neither can they be cowed into accepting on faith the results of decision models or computer systems. They want to know the reason for the answer that is proposed and how the system manages to develop a forecast which they intuitively know is difficult to make.

If managers have this level of understanding of *how and why* the system does what it does, they are much more likely to use it and to have faith in the decisions which they base on it. If not, they will develop their own systems, however unsophisticated, in which they do have faith, and use them.

The author knows of several companies where middle-level managers and operatives rely on black loose-leaf notebooks ("butcher books") in which they manually record the same transactions which are automatically tracked and recorded by a computer system. They do this because they have faith in their own system and do not understand the computerized one. Their sense of purpose in doing a good job and in not being misled by a system leads them to subvert it, at great cost to the organization since only one of the two systems is really necessary.

Understanding the how and why of the MMIS will also enable the manager to feel that he is in control rather than, as often is the case, that he is controlled by the system. The manager who understands, for example, that invoices are coded by county can confidently request sales analyses by county even if they have not previously been supplied to him. He may be told that some time and cost will be involved, if this capability has not already been programmed, but he will not be led to making unreasonable requests, such as asking for sales analyses by township or city. In the latter case, when he is told that it cannot be done, the uninformed manager usually feels put upon by the system and constrained by it. This can lead to the development of an unreasonable antipathy toward the MMIS and its proponents merely because it cannot do everything. The informed manager will recognize this in advance and not be put in the position of making unreasonable requests of a system that is necessarily limited in its capabilities.

The Nature of Managerial Work

Management understanding is closely tied in with analyst understanding. Information system analysts, because of their training and experience, usually have little understanding of what managers do and how they do it. This, therefore, leads to another principle of MMIS design—*that systems should be designed in conformance with a realistic model of the nature of managerial work.*

Managers and organizational analysts, unlike information system analysts, do know something about the nature of managerial work. For instance, Mintzberg has provided the following six characteristics of managerial work based on empirical evidence: [9]

1. The manager performs a great quantity of work at an unrelenting pace.
2. Managerial activity is characterized by variety, fragmentation, and brevity.
3. Managers prefer issues that are current, specific, and ad hoc.
4. The manager sits between his organization and a network of contacts.
5. The manager demonstrates a strong preference for the verbal media.
6. Despite the preponderance of obligations, the manager appears to be in control of his own affairs.

Of course, these six characteristics do not represent the definitive understanding of the nature of managerial work. However, they are of obvious value to the systems designer, especially when it is recognized that he is likely to be oriented, by virtue of his personality and training, to very different feelings, beliefs, and operating habits when it comes to work. For instance, most analysts are not used to working in an environment in which activity can be characterized by variety, fragmentation, and brevity. Indeed, if such were the case, complex systems would probably never be successfully developed!

If the analyst projects his own model of carefully thought-out decisions, written media, etc., onto the manager and then designs a system for this "ideal" manager, it is unlikely to be a very useful system for the typical manager characterized by Mintzberg. [10]

The Importance of Top Management Support

Efforts in developing computerized information systems are costly and time consuming. The strategy for development is therefore very important, for like any

---

[9] Henry Mintzberg, "Managerial Work: Analysis from Observation," *Management Science,* October 1971.

[10] See also Henry Mintzberg, "The Manager's Job: Folklore and Fact," *Harvard Business Review,* July–August 1975.

prolonged and costly activity, MMIS developments are prime targets for cost cutting, especially in times of economic downturns.

While some of the other major projects in which a company may also be involved are susceptible to postponement, MMIS development efforts are unique in that they do not age well. Many of the activities involved in developing an information system are artistic in nature, despite the fact that such systems appear to be the epitome of scientific and engineering achievement. Because of this, they are not easily taken up by other people once they have been set aside. For instance, a partially completed computer program is unlikely to be finished once the programmer has been transferred.

It is imperative, therefore, that the continued support of top management be achieved. As Schewe has said: [11]

> . . . top management must be given tangible evidence of the value of the marketing information system. Central to the development of a marketing-oriented information system is a total commitment from top executives within the firm and also within the marketing area itself. This commitment must, naturally, involve heavy financial commitment—but equally important is top management's leadership in developing an appreciation of the need and desirability of a marketing information system, an orientation that will filter down through the organization's ranks. In order to obtain this commitment, the initial MIS efforts should be focused upon providing immediate and tangible returns on the corporate investment in the marketing information system.

Schewe provides both a design principle and a strategy for achieving it. The principle is that the achievement of top management support is an essential ingredient for success in any complex, costly and time-consuming activity such as MMIS design and development. The strategy for achieving this support, as suggested by Schewe, is to *provide intermediate valuable outputs along the way to the development of the overall system.*

There are few top managers who are willing to wait many months and watch large amounts of resources being expended on an MMIS development effort on the basis of a promise that the MMIS will, in the end, be worth the wait. Those few that may appear to be so willing are likely to have a change of heart should business conditions falter and resources become tighter. Thus, if the MMIS designer is to avoid project termination, postponement, or slowdown, he must achieve firm top management support by developing useful system outputs prior to the completion of the entire system. In this way, managers can be shown the tangible benefits of the system while the design and development process is still underway. The support thereby derived will usually ensure that the MMIS development effort will be given high priority and brought to fulfillment.

---

[11] C. D. Schewe, "Management Information Systems in Marketing—A Promise Not Yet Realized," *Management Informatics,* vol. 3, no. 5 (1974).

Modular Design

The concept of modular design has come into prominence throughout various systems-oriented fields in recent years. Modular design means that the overall system is broken up into modules—subsets which perform identifiable functions, provide specified output, and which can, to some degree, "stand on their own."

When systems are designed on such a modular basis, some modules can be designed, developed, and fully operationalized while other modules are still in the early design stages. This has many advantages, not the least of which are the following:

1. The significantly lesser complexity of any module as compared with the overall system
2. The motivational benefits derived from achieving the interim goals which are represented by each module
3. The opportunity to provide managers with interim payoffs in terms of the capabilities provided by each module, rather than requiring them to await the completion of the overall system

A modularized MMIS might be constructed on a variety of different bases. If the system is being constructed from scratch, transaction processing might be given initial focus. In effect, the transaction processing subsystem would be defined as the initial module to be completed. Once this module is operating, attention would be turned to other modules, each chosen to (1) be related to previously completed modules in a way that builds on or amplifies their outputs; and (2) have outputs which have value that will be recognized by top management.

Of course, bases for modularization other than a hierarchical one may also be used. The other common basis is functional. Using such an approach, the designer might choose to first develop a sales module which would involve all levels of sales information from transaction reporting through the development of sales models for the support of sales management decision making. Then, once the sales module is operational, the MMIS developers might turn their attention to other functional modules such as an advertising module, a new product module, or a marketing cost module.

Subsystem integration

Associated with the idea of modular design is the critical need for *system integration*. This merely means that every module must be fully integrated with previously developed modules in order that the modules be mutually supportive.

While this seems like an obvious thing, it is noted here because it is often violated in practice.

For instance, consider the bank which has routinized a wide variety of transactions through the development of computer systems for checking, credit cards, loans, etc., only to find that these distinct systems do not provide the capability for providing salient management information. The marketing vice-president, in fulfilling his role of developing new customers, would like to conduct a campaign to sell new services to people who are currently customers of a limited set of services. He reasons that a checking customer has a higher potential for buying a credit card than does someone with no existing ties with the bank. However, his various systems have no low cost capability for providing him with a list of the services used by each customer. This is so because the various systems were developed independently without concern for such interactions. Moreover, since one individual may be listed in various systems in terms of various forms of his name (e.g., last- first- middle versus last- first- middle initial), there is not even any reliable way of performing manual analysis to provide accurate information at reasonable cost.

The cause of this incongruous situation is the ignoring of systems integration during the design of the various subsystems, each of which may itself be productive and effective. The difficulty is in the system interactions, so that the manager who wishes to avoid such pitfalls should be cognizant of these interrelationships and their potential for both great harm and great benefit.

Evolutionary Design

Most often the MMIS will probably be developed on a modular basis rather than as a simplistic total system. Most assuredly, it should be developed in accordance with the *principle of evolutionary systems design, namely, that the system should be designed to allow for future evolution of the system; in other words, in a fashion which presumes that the system will never really be completed, but will constantly be undergoing further modular development, system changes, and modifications.* If this is successfully done, the system will never become obsolete because it will be completely renewed and revitalized over its normal life cycle.

This principle of evolutionary design is of particular importance in inflationary times when large-scale systems become so expensive. In other days, one could afford to throw out the old system and develop a new one from scratch. Indeed, in a disposable society, even sophisticated computer systems become throwaways in some sense. Now, few companies adopt that view and most desire evolutionary design which promises a long life for the basic MMIS investment.

Disaggregated data files

The key to evolutionary systems design is the disaggregated data file. Although the term is probably unfamiliar and seemingly out of place in a management-oriented MMIS discussion, the idea of a disaggregated data file is simple enough. Such a file is merely one in which data are maintained in the time sequence in which they were obtained or generated. New inputs do not replace, or are not combined with, old data. This permits the development of a detailed history for many elements of information, some of which may have no apparent purpose at the moment.

For instance, a disaggregated customer file would contain a record of each transaction rather than just a record of current ones and/or of cumulative totals. Such a record has obvious value when any misunderstandings arise with the customer, but it also has value for analyses which may not currently be performed in the organization.

A system design using disaggregated data files, along with records of variable rather than fixed length, is susceptible to evolutionary change. One without such characteristics may be changed only through a system "revolution."

Summary

While there are no eternally and universally valid principles of MMIS design, our level of understanding about what it takes to develop a good MMIS and about those factors which have contributed to the development of poor MMIS has increased in recent years to the point where some principles may be tentatively stated. Such principles represent standards by which MMIS design processes should be preliminarily judged.

One most important principle is that the MMIS should provide the manager with the minimum amount of relevant information that he needs to perform his job effectively, and no more. Exception reporting, in which the manager is routinely given only reports dealing with exceptional circumstances, is one way of achieving this goal.

Another principle is that the system must satisfy the perceived informational needs of its user-managers. Any system that does not meet these needs will not be used, at least for the purposes and in the manner that was intended. A criterion of user-oriented systems optimality, which judges a system both in terms of its technical performance and its likelihood of being accepted and used by managers, may not always lead to the development of the technically "best" system, but it is likely to lead to an effective system which is used as intended.

While this book focuses on the modern variety of MMIS which features management decision support as a primary goal, this variety of system must be developed in a fashion consistent with the cost-effectiveness principle. This means that decision support should be pursued only so far as it results in gains which more than offset the costs of providing the support.

The principle of manager-analyst cooperative design suggests that neither analysts nor managers are capable of designing an effective MMIS independently of one another. Thus, a cooperative design effort is essential.

A cooperative design effort is also a good way to implement the principle that managers must understand the MMIS if they are to be willing to use it and to control it rather than to be controlled by it.

The converse is also an important design principle—that systems should be designed in accordance with a realistic model of the nature of managerial work. This means that analysts and designers must be provided with knowledge about the nature of the manager's job and, hence, the limitations which this places on the MMIS.

That top management support is a necessary ingredient for MMIS success is another critical design principle. One effective strategy for implementing this principle is to provide intermediate valuable outputs as the design-development process proceeds. This is consistent with the idea of *modular design,* since various modules can be completed and put into operation before the overall MMIS is completed.

An evolutionary design principle is also basic to the development of a good MMIS. This design concept recognizes that the system will constantly be undergoing revision and adaptation. Thus, an MMIS plan represents a goal devoutly to be sought but, perhaps, never fully achieved because unforeseeable changes in the outside world will make revisions to the system necessary. If each module or element is developed with such changes in mind, the evolution of the MMIS will be facilitated. If not, the system will need to be scrapped and, at great cost, replaced by an entirely different system.

EXERCISES

1. What is the worth of MMIS principles if they are not deemed universally valid?

2. In your own words, tell what is meant by "relevant" information. Now define the same concept in terms that are decision-model-oriented.

3. What is exception reporting? If a system were *totally* based on exception reporting and nothing were out of control, what would happen? In such a system, what would happen if everything were out of control?

4. Despite the principle related to user-based design, Chapter 6 says, "If systems were slavishly designed to conform to managerial criteria, the likely result would be organizational stagnation." What does that statement mean? What are its implications for the system designer?

5. Give some examples of systems that might be accepted and rejected if the following principle is applied: It is far better to develop an improved system that is implemented than to develop one that is theoretically optimal, but which is not implemented.

6. What might be the impact on managers of a system that was designed to present them with exception information about out of control processes using displays of cartoon characters telling them that they had better "do something" ?

7. Why must an MMIS be oriented toward providing similar information to *classes* of managers, rather than to each individual manager?

8. Why is cost savings a poor sole basis for judging the worth of a proposed MMIS?

9. Describe the process which often occurs after managers and analysts have had a meeting to kick off a new MMIS design and pledged to work together to design the system.

10. Managers must understand the MMIS. Why is this so?

11. Give an illustration of how each of Mintzberg's six characteristics of managerial work can be transformed into an MMIS design characteristic or principle.

REFERENCES

Ackoff, R. L. "Management Misinformation Systems." *Management Science,* December 1967.

Amstutz, A. E. "The Marketing Executive and Management Information Systems." In Haas, R., ed., *Science, Technology and Marketing,* American Marketing Association, 1966.

Axelrod, J. N. "14 Rules for Building an MIS." *Journal of Advertising Research,* June 1970.

Berenson, C. "Marketing Information Systems." *Journal of Marketing,* October 1969.

Cox, D. F., and Good, R. E. "How to Build a Marketing Information System." *Harvard Business Review,* May–June 1967.

Dickson, G. W., and Simmons, J. K. "The Behavioral Side of MIS." *Business Horizons,* August 1970.

Ein-Dor, P. "Parallel Strategy for MIS." *Journal of Systems Management,* March 1975, pp. 30–35.

Gibson, L. D., et al. "An Evolutionary Approach to Marketing Information Systems. *Journal of Marketing,* April 1973.

Ghymn, Kyung, Il, and King, William R. "Design of Strategic Planning MIS." *OMEGA,* 1976.

Groyson, C. J., Jr. "Management Science and Business Practice." *Harvard Business Review,* July–Aug. 1973, pp. 41–48.

Gupta, R. "Information Manager: His Role in Corporate Management." *Data Management,* July 1974, pp. 26–29.

Hammond, J. "The Roles of Manager and Management Scientist in Successful Implementation." *Sloan Management Review,* Winter 1974, pp. 1–24.

Heany, D. F. "Education: The Critical Link in Getting Managers to Use Management Systems." *Interfaces,* May 1972, pp. 1–7.

Industrial Marketing, November 1966. "Why Industrial Marketers Aren't Using Computers."

7

Developing the General Design
of the MMIS

The process of developing any information system involves four distinct phases: (1) project planning, (2) development of the general systems design, (3) development of the detailed systems design and (4) implementation and operation. These steps are performed roughly in the order listed, although, in a very real sense, all should be going on during the entire design development cycle. Perhaps the best way to think of the sequential relationship of the various phases is that the beginnings of each phase take place in the order noted, but the phases themselves take place in parallel.[1]

Project planning delineates both the work to be done in the design and development process and also who is to perform each task, when each is to be completed, and the resources which are to be allocated to each task. This project management aspect of systems design is extremely important, but we shall defer discussion of it until a later chapter in order to concentrate first on the primary phases of systems design. This will permit us to develop a greater understanding of the system being developed before we concern ourselves with the planning and management of the systems development effort.

The *general design* of the system is the broad-scale abstract description of the MMIS to be developed. This description is in terms of system objectives, limitations, information to be processed, general system flow, major subsystems and their inputs and outputs, etc. In effect, the general design is a broad road map within which the detailed design is developed.

The *detailed design* of the system involves the precise prescription for subsystem and module inputs, outputs, software, hardware, flows, models, operating systems, etc. In effect, it is the final system which is to be put into operation.

Implementation and operation involve the installation and testing of the system, the development of manuals and other operating instructions, the hiring and training of personnel to operate the system and all other diverse things that need to be done to get the system going.

In this chapter we give primary attention to the development of the general design of the system. The general design phase is made up of a number of subphases, including system planning (as distinct from *project* planning), the determination of system objectives, the identification of system constraints and boundaries, and general system specifications in terms of subsystems, information flow, subsystem inputs and outputs, and subsystem relationships.

---

[1] R. G. Murdick, "MIS Development Procedures," *Journal of Systems Management,* December 1970, pp. 22–26, gives a compilation of the various phases of the system development process as seen by various authors.

System Planning and Establishing
System Objectives

Any enterprise, be it the establishment of a business or an MMIS, is best begun with the identification of the things which the enterprise will try to accomplish— its objectives. These objectives, in part, comprise the *plan* which guides the development of the enterprise.

MMIS objectives often arise out of problems which exist in the organization. Managers will have identified particular operating or decision areas which they believe to be deficient, or other difficulties will have arisen which lead to the consideration of a solution in the form of a new information system.

While such problems involving critical incidents are perfectly appropriate for generating interest in, and support for, an MMIS, they should not be allowed to constrain the MMIS's objectives and general design. The old cliché that managers usually identify symptoms rather than real problems is, in this context, very valid. The problems or difficulties which are the initial motivators for considering a new MMIS usually reflect deeper needs and deficiencies which can be identified only after some study. For instance, a problem of "orders not getting shipped on time" may be traceable to delays in submission by salespeople, to lack of inventory, to poor coordination between the warehouse and the shipping department, to poor selection of carriers or to any of dozens of other possible *real problems*. Late shipment is really a symptom of an underlying problem which can be identified only after a thorough systems analysis has been performed. But, more importantly, to develop an MMIS which is aimed at correcting the problem of late shipments without understanding what the real problem may be, is utter folly and ineffectual. Such a new MMIS is unlikely to clear up the problem if it is developed on the basis of a lack of understanding of what the problem really is.

Thus, problems, as identified by management, should not be allowed to constrain the development of broad objectives for an MMIS. Such problems are merely suggestive of opportunities which exist for organizational improvements through the development of information systems.

General systems planning—conceptual approach

The question which naturally arises is how a problem situation and organization can be analyzed in order to establish worthy system objectives. A general answer to this question has been provided by the author and his colleague [2] in their specification of a conceptual approach to strategic systems planning. It is based on the

[2] William R. King and David I. Cleland, "A New Approach to Strategic Systems Planning," *Business Horizons*, August 1975.

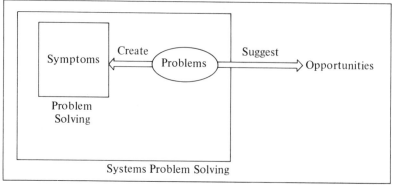

FIGURE 7-1 **Three views of problem solving**

three views of problem solving which are described in Figure 7-1. This figure shows the relationships between problems, symptoms, and opportunities and defines three levels of analysis which may be applied to them.

The first is *traditional problem solving,* which involves the scientific approach of cutting the problem down to size by simplifying it and treating only its salient features. While this is a necessary approach to the ultimate solution of any problem, it suffers operationally from its implicit assumption that the right problem has been identified. Often, this is not the case and the traditional mode of problem solving may lead to solving the wrong problem or to the development of a system which does not resolve the symptoms.[3] Indeed, the domain of traditional problem solving is shown in the figure to deal largely with *symptoms,* since the parochial nature of the analytic process and the organizations which deal with problems are such that only narrow viewpoints are taken of most problem contexts.

Of course, many may view this drawing of a correlation between problem solving and symptoms as an exaggeration; but within the context of society, there are, in reality, few problems which get dealt with at anything other than a symptomatic level, even when the process required to do so is simple logic rather than insight or clairvoyance. For instance, an American city spent years in debate over an airport extension for the existing public transit system and, on finally building the system, found itself faced with a proposal for relocating the airport because of a forecast of early inadequacy and the high cost of expansion at the existing site. Such a sequence of events clearly indicates the restrictions placed on problem solving both by our traditional analytical methods and by organizational constraints which do not motivate people to look beyond the bounds of the

[3] I. I. Mitroff, and T. R. Featheringham, "On Systemic Problem Solving and the Error of the Third Kind," *Behavioral Science,* vol. 19, no. 6 (November 1974).

problem as presented, or beyond the scope of their own organization and personal responsibilities.

Figure 7-1 also shows *systems problem solving* in terms of a focus on the broader domain of symptoms *and* problems. This has been the concern of systems-oriented managers and authors in the last decade, and it is a clear improvement over nonsystematic approaches.

The need for a systems approach to problem-solving is based on a variety of characteristics of the problems with which managers deal and the processes which may feasibly be used to deal with them. The dictionary's definition of a *system* in terms of "an assemblage of interacting and interdependent parts forming a unified whole" should probably have the words "interacting" and "interdependent" in italics, because in practice the utility of the systems viewpoint depends on these characteristics. This is so because there is no particular value to the taking of a systems view of a system of non-interacting independent parts. Such parts might just as well be treated separately since they have no effect on one another.

Thus, the interactions and interdependencies among the elements of a complex system are major complicating factors which necessitate an overall systems viewpoint. Such interactions and interdependencies are, of course, common in all social systems.

Another important dimension of complex problems is that referred to as *second-order consequences*. These consequences are those that appear subsequent to, or as a result of, the immediate and obvious consequences of an action. One can, for instance, view the process of technological innovation as one in which many new technologies have produced immediate and obvious consequences which were beneficial to society, but also produced later second-order consequences which were not so beneficial. The automobile thereby produced inexpensive transportation for the masses, but also changed society in various ways that many believe to be negative through such things as the elimination of neighborhood togetherness, providing the opportunity for greater sexual freedom among the young, and pre-empting the growth of mass transit. In addition to these consequences, the automobile contributed to major societal problems such as pollution, the solution of which is at least partially responsible for yet another problem—an "energy crisis." The *chain of effects* in going from a problem to immediate consequences, then to second-order consequences and newly-created problems is one of the pervasive characteristics of modern social systems. Quite literally, in such systems, everything depends on everything else, and often in ways so complex and roundabout that it is difficult to understand the interrelationships.

As the figure shows, the domain of problems can be further extended to encompass opportunities in the *strategic systems planning*. For instance, a major fast food chain is faced with a peak load problem of tremendous magnitude. Its facilities are stretched to the breaking point at the lunch and dinner hours, and there is plenty of slack time at other hours. This problem of unused resources is viewed as an opportunity to introduce new items on its menu which will have special appeal at nonpeak hours (breakfast items, snack items, and nighttime specialties). Another company uses the major "problems" of society and business—consumerism, pollution control, etc.—as a basis for a formal study of market opportunities which may be related to these phenomena. From this study, it concluded that it has the expertise to make a profit in several lines of business which will aid society and simultaneously reduce the image of business as a creator, rather than a solver, of societal problems.

In the former case, a single creative mind *could have* turned the problem into an opportunity. In the latter case, substantial study, data gathering and analysis were required beyond the capacity of any individual. In both cases, the likelihood of achieving the transition from problem to opportunity was greatly enhanced by an operational process of applying systems ideas to planning.

General systems planning—operational approach

To operationalize this strategic systems planning involves a four-stage process: (1) defining the organization in systems terms, (2) delineating goals for each organizational element and claimant, (3) identifying organizational objectives, and (4) developing system objectives.

Defining the organization in systems terms. To define the organization in systems terms means that one explicitly goes through the process of blowing up the problem. The most important element in doing this has to do with explicitly describing every relevant clientele group and organizational claimant in terms which are meaningful and, hopefully, measurable.

Clientele groups, sometimes referred to as stakeholders to distinguish them from the legal owners of corporations, are those who have a stake in the activities and future of an organization. Thus, workers, stockholders, suppliers, and customers are invariably relevant clientele groups of a business enterprise, and the impact of organizational decisions on *all* of them must be considered in a rational systems approach to management.

Delineating goals for organizational claimants. Each individual, department, and claimant group has goals related to the nature of their claim on the organization which affect the outcome and determine the effectiveness of organizational decisions. An explicit and objective consideration of these claimants and the nature of their claims permits the systems viewpoint to be adopted and provides the opportunity for the kind of measurement which is so critical to prediction and decision making. Table 7-1 shows how some stakeholder claims may be made explicit for a business firm.

TABLE 7-1 * Stakeholders and their Claims

Stockholders	Participate in distribution of profits, additional stock offerings, assets on liquidation; vote of stock, inspection of company books, transfer of stock, election of board of directors, and such additional rights as established in the contract with corporations.
Creditors	Participate in legal proportion of interest payments due and return of principal from the investment. Security of pledged assets; relative priority in event of liquidation. Participate in certain management and owner prerogatives if certain conditions exist within the company (such as default of interest payments).
Employees	Economic, social, and psychological satisfaction in the place of employment. Freedom from effects of arbitrary and capricious behavior on the part of company officials. Share in fringe benefits. Freedom to join union and participate in collective bargaining. Individual freedom in offering up their services through an employment contract. Adequate working conditions.
Customers	Service provided for the product; technical data to use with the product; suitable warranties; spare parts to support the product during customer use; R & D leading to product improvement; facilitation of consumer credit.
Supplier	Continuing source of business; timely consummation of trade credit obligations; professional relationship in contracting for, purchasing, and receiving goods and services.
Governments	Taxes (income, property, etc.), fair competition, and adherence to the letter and intent of public policy dealing with the requirements of ''fair and free'' competition. Legal obligation for businessmen (and business organizations) to obey antitrust laws.
Union	Recognition as the negotiating agent for the employees. Opportunity to perpetuate the union as a participant in the business organization.
Competitors	Norms established by society and the industry for competitive conduct. Business ''statesmanship'' on the part of contemporaries.
Local communities	Place of productive and healthful employment in the local community. Participation of the company officials in community affairs. Regular employment, fair play. Purchase of reasonable portion of the products of the local community, interest in and support of local government and cultural and charity projects by the company.
General public	Company participation in and contribution to the governmental process of society as a whole; creative communications between governmental and business units designed for reciprocal understanding; bear fair proportion of the burden of government and society. Fair price for products and advancement of the state-of-the art in the technology which the product line offers.

* Adapted with permission from David I. Cleland and William R. King, *Systems Analysis and Project Management,* 2d ed. (New York: McGraw-Hill, 1975).

Identifying organizational objectives. Once clientele objectives have been delineated, the organization's objectives should be identified. These objectives may be stated in the strategic plan or long-range plan which has been developed to guide the organization.

Sometimes these objectives will be quite simple: to achieve a 10 percent compounded sales growth and a return on investment of 15 percent. Other organizations will have a complex set of objectives, many of which may not be stated in easily measurable terms such as to be recognized as a leader in the industry. In any case, each of the organization's objectives serves both as a guide for the MMIS, since presumably its ultimate purpose is to aid the organization in achieving its objectives, and as an opportunity, since the MMIS may be able to provide information which will help the organization's top managers to assess how well they are doing in achieving basic objectives.

Developing MMIS Objectives. Deriving MMIS objectives on the basis of the previous steps *recognizes the intrinsic relationship between clientele objectives, organizational objectives, and system objectives.* As shown in Figure 7-2, the diverse objectives of clientele groups inevitably affect the objectives and strategy of the firm. The figure shows a few of the firm's objectives. An analysis of them shows their clear relationship to clientele objectives:

Objectives for per share earnings relate to the objectives of stockholders, creditors (who wish to see the firm remain strong and financially stable), suppliers, employees, etc.

Objectives of social responsibility relate to the objectives of the general public, government, public interest groups, etc.

Objectives for product quality and safety relate to the objectives of customers, government regulatory agencies, etc.

These organizational objectives can be translated into system objectives in fairly direct ways. One obvious way is that *the MMIS must provide information on the degree to which various company and clientele objectives are being achieved.* This can be done through identifying measurable quantities which reflect each objective and by incorporating these measures into the system specifications. For instance, product quality and safety objectives can be monitored through measurable quantities such as the following:

Number of warranty repairs

Number of safety-related warranty repairs

Number of call back programs (such as those conducted by auto manufacturers)

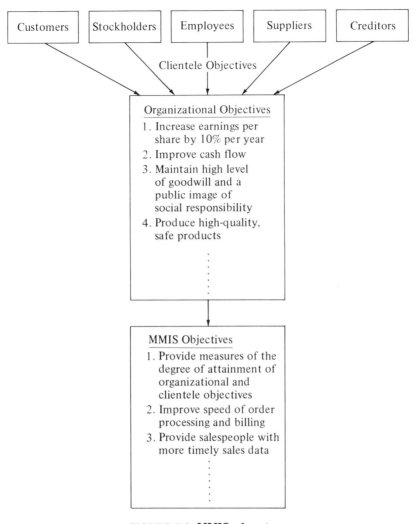

FIGURE 7-2 MMIS planning

Number of quality and safety lawsuits filed against the company

Number of inquiries related to quality and safety from government regulatory agencies

Brand loyalty data reflecting brand switching for quality and safety reasons

Newspaper and magazine reports related to product quality and safety

Other system objectives may be less directly related to clientele and organizational objectives, but they are nonetheless important. For instance, the following objectives have been given by Murdick and Ross for a billing subsystem of an MMIS: [4]

Provide input to other subsystems

Improve cash flow

Maintain customer goodwill

Timely invoice processing

Keep salespeople informed

With the exception of the technical first objective, these subsystem objectives relate directly to organizational and clientele objectives:

Cash flow relates to an organizational objective to improve overall cash flow, which is in turn related to objectives of stockholders, creditors, etc.

Customer goodwill relates to an organizational objective, which, in turn, relates to customer objectives.

Timely invoice processing relates to ''cash flow'' objectives as well as to customer objectives.

Keeping salespeople informed relates to employee objectives.

Thus, *MMIS objectives can be directly developed from a study and analysis of clientele and organizational objectives and strategy.* If this is done, it will make sure the MMIS is integrated into the organization and not merely appended to it. It will also increase the likelihood of acceptance of the MMIS, since it will be designed directly to aid the organization in doing its job. Such a system is likely to be viewed positively by nonmarketing managers as well as by those in marketing. A system which is not tied into the organization and its objectives is, conversely, likely to be viewed as a highly specialized system which exists solely for the support of the marketing function. Such a system cannot be expected to receive the strong support of nonmarketing managers since it neither directly helps them in their functions nor directly supports the overall organization in the pursuit of its objectives.

System Constraints and MMIS Design Characteristics

Just as it is important to think big in taking a systems viewpoint that is not narrowly restricted to symptoms, it is also important to define specifically the boundaries of the MMIS and the constraints under which it must be designed and

[4] R. G. Murdick and J. E. Ross, *Information Systems for Modern Management,* 2d ed. (Englewood Cliffs, N.J.: Prentice-Hall, 1975), p. 205.

operated. Such constraints serve to define the scope of the system as well as its nature.

Policy constraints

Every organization has policies—statements of acceptable and unacceptable strategies and activities. The policies may directly bear on the MMIS and other information systems, such as would policies relating to decentralized computer support and the necessity to cost justify new system projects.

A policy may primarily relate to business operations while still having impact on the MMIS. For instance, a policy of growth through acquisition suggests that the MMIS should have the capability for identifying potential acquisition candidates *on the basis,* at least, *of marketing characteristics.* Which firms, for instance, share the same distribution channels and hence offer the potential for synergy if we acquire them? Which firms have products which would enable us to fill out our product line?

If it is the policy of the firm to develop new services which may be sold to the customer along with the product, the MMIS may become a vehicle for the development of such information services. For instance, the MMIS data on various industries' sales and usage patterns may be repackaged for sale to customers, or mailing lists may be developed as a "new product," based on the MMIS files.

Personnel constraints

A major area for consideration in developing the general MMIS design has to do with the nature of the system. Is the system to be one involving a direct managerial interface, say with cathode ray tube (CRT) displays on the desks of managers, or is it one which will provide human intervention between the system and the manager? Is the system one which will rely on business-oriented computer languages such as COBOL or is a "natural language" a requirement so that managers will find it easier to communicate with the system?

The answers to such questions about the nature of the system depend importantly on the nature of the people in the organization. It would be foolhardy to design a sophisticated system for managers who had not had previous computer training and experience. The result would inevitably be the creation of fear and trepidation about the system in the minds of the managers and their consequent mistrust and lack of use of the system.

There must be a match between the character and capability of the system users and the system itself if the system is to be used for its intended purpose. While this need may not always please the system designer, who is generally "turned on" only if he is allowed to design the most sophisticated system which is feasible, it will lead to systems which achieve *organizational* goals.

Cost constraints

The most severe constraint under which a MMIS is designed is a cost constraint. Generally, the budget limitation is known in the form of a "ballpark estimate" at the outset of a design process. While this estimate should not be taken to be the unquestioned maximum, it should also not be ignored in the development of the general MMIS design. This admonition may seem obvious to the ininitiated, but it is apparently not so obvious to system designers, who often develop system designs which go far beyond the limits of available funds. This process of system design which gets carried away from the reality of available funds is bad for some apparent and some subtle reasons.

In another context, Enthoven [5] has given a description of two ways in which a house may be designed. This "homey" example well illustrates both some of the difficulties inherent in overdesign and the proper procedure for taking the available budget into account while not treating it as an irrevocable maximum.

> Suppose that I want to buy a house . . . First, I determine my housing requirements without any consideration of costs. I count up the rooms I require: I need a bedroom for myself, one for each of my children, and one for my parents or other guests who come to visit us occasionally. I need a study because I occasionally bring some of my work home with me and need a quiet place to work. My wife needs a sewing room. I need a pool in the basement because my doctor has told me that I must swim every day if I don't want to have another operation on my back. Now, you might laugh when I say that I have to have a pool in my basement, but I can validate that requirement. I can argue for it very convincingly. I can produce a doctor's certificate, and you can't prove to me that I don't need that pool. Moreover, I work at the Pentagon and I work long hours. Therefore, I need to live within five minutes drive of the Pentagon. When I put this all together, I find that I have established a requirement for a house that costs a hundred thousand dollars. Having done that, I review my financial situation and find that I am only able to spend about $30,000. So what do I do? If I am operating under the old concept, I take the $100,000 design and I slice off 70 percent of it and what's left is my house.

> Now, clearly that's not a very sensible way to design a house. I might find that I left off the bathroom, or included the bathroom, but left off the plumbing that is required to make it work. Yet that's a pretty fair description of the way that the Department of Defense did its business. We found in 1961 that we had Army Divisions without adequate airlift or other means of mobility and with far from adequate supplies of equipment. We had tactical air wings without supplies of nonnuclear ordnance, and numerous other similar problems. In effect, we had bought a lot of houses without the bathrooms or the plumbing.

[5] Alain C. Enthoven, address before the Aviation and Space Writers Convention, Miami, Fla., 25 May 1964.

Thus, as Enthoven describes, if one does not take explicit account of costs and benefits, but rather thinks solely in terms of requirements, he is likely to be left holding the bag. If it takes a $100,000 house to meet my requirements and I can afford only a $30,000 house, I clearly should not just chop off some features of the $100,000 house until it costs $30,000. Rather, I should begin to plan with the $30,000 in mind. Enthoven described this process as follows: [6]

> The rational economic way of buying a house . . . is to consider alternative balanced programs each of which yields the most effectiveness possible within a budget that corresponds approximately to the availability of our resources. If I think that I have about $30,000 to spend on a house, I should consider several alternative houses each optimized for my purposes within financial limits such as $28,000, $30,000, $32,000, and perhaps $34,000 and then I should ask myself whether the extra advantages associated with the more expensive houses are worth the extra financial sacrifices I would have to make to pay for one. It's altogether possible that they might be. For example, a larger house might have a recreation room, and this might enable me to economize elsewhere on recreation.

Specification of the General MMIS Design

There has been a good deal of controversy in the field of system design as to how large a role should be played by the existing system in the design of a new system. Proponents of a fresh approach or idealized system design argue that the new system should be designed quite independently of any system which may currently exist in the organization. Others take the position that this is inefficient and that it violates basic informational principles by ignoring the information that is contained in the existing system.

The approach to general system specification outlined here encompasses both these points of view. Moreover, it focuses directly on the MMIS design principles that were outlined in the previous chapter.

The process for the general design involves a series of steps. [7] As in most such processes, the sequencing of steps is in terms of the initiation rather than the execution of each. Thus, step 1 *begins* before step 2, but because of the implicit feedback loops and interdependencies in the process, step 1 may not end prior to the end of step 2.

There are six steps in the process:

---

[6] Ibid.

[7] Portions of this description are adapted with permission from the author's paper with David I. Cleland; William R. King and David I. Cleland: "The Design of Management Information Systems: An Information Analysis Approach," *Management Science,* November 1975.

1. Identification of user sets and interfacing organizations
2. Identification of decision areas
3. Definition of decision areas
4. Development of a descriptive model of the system
5. Development of a normative model of the system
6. Development of a consensus model of the system

Identification of user sets and interfacing organizations

The user sets for an MIS, the sets consisting of those managers who are designated to be the primary users of the system's output, are in part specified by the stated objectives of the system. Such objectives must be clearly defined prior to embarking on the specification of an MMIS general design.

The user sets are initially defined by the analyst, using the statement of objectives for the MMIS, organization charts, job descriptions, and other documents as guides. They are defined so as to permit the system design to be oriented toward a reasonable number of user groups, each of which is treated as a homogeneous entity.

Often, the system objectives reflect the recognition that past inadequacies are largely due to a lack of relevant information. Most of the information or data that are currently processed by the organization's information system are descriptive of the past history of the internal organizational subsystem. Most of the information is outdated and inward directed. To be useful, such information must be prospective and focused toward those environmental and competitive elements of the organization that will most critically affect its future.

Because of this, the analyst must consider external interfacing organizations as well as internal users. These organizations are defined in terms of specific informational inputs and outputs, that is, those organizations with which information is communicated in support of, or as a result of, the functions which the MIS is to support.

Identification of decision areas

The next step in the information analysis process involves the identification of decision areas. This step is initiated by the analyst on the basis of existing knowledge and refined by him through discussion with the appropriate managers who will be the users of the system.

Table 7-2 shows such a decision inventory related to the planning function of one organization. It represents one possible delineation of some of the critical decision areas involved in the planning process in any organization.

TABLE 7-2 Decision Areas

Policy formation—internal
Policy formation—external
Direction of operations
Organizing activities
Budget
Tactical Planning
New programs
Training
Personnel selection
Allocation of resources
Research
External coordination
Internal coordination

Other categorizations could be used as well. In fact, during the process of developing such an inventory, the analyst will usually begin from a theoretical point of view based on his highly abstracted view of the organization and then proceed to revise his inventory based on discussions with executives and members of the user sets. This process serves to provide a good theoretical foundation and to make sure major omissions are avoided, while at the same time avoiding the problems of confusing terminology and overlapping decision areas.

Definition of decision areas

After decision areas have been identified, they must be specified in detail. The discussions held with executives and the members of the user sets, as outlined in the previous step, will assist greatly in achieving the desired level of specificity. These discussions serve a secondary purpose as well—the obtaining of support and acceptance by the people on whom ultimate success will depend.

The process involved here is, therefore, much the same as that of the previous step except that the decision areas are broken into decision elements on the basis of their (1) homogeneity, (2) need for common informational input, and (3) performance by a single individual or unit. In all cases, these assessments must be made on rather loose grounds, since rigorous formal criteria are probably unwarranted at this preliminary definitional stage.

For instance, the row labels at the left side of Table 7-3 describe various decision elements associated with one broad decision area from Table 7-2. Thus, all of the tasks which are listed at the left side of Table 7-3 have been specified as the detailed functions that must be performed within *one* of the decision areas which the MMIS is to support.

TABLE 7-3 LRC System Model

	Marketing VP (1)	Executive VP (2)	Comptroller (3)	Department Manager (4)	Sales Manager (5)	Product Managers (6)	Marketing Analyst (7)	Salespeople (8)	Field Sales Department (9)	Legal Department (10)	Production Department (11)
Analysis of routine complaints				A	C_4	S	E	C_7	7^i	7^i	
Observation of field practices				A	S	E	C_6				
Complaint analysis				A	S	E	C_6		6^i	6^i	
Warranty analysis				A	E	C			5^i	5^i	5^i
Call back analysis				A	S	E	C_6		6^i	6^i	6^i
Analysis of new legislation				A	S	E	C_6		6^i	6^i	6^i
Issue clarification and definition				A	S	E	C_6				
Selection of alternatives				A	E	C_5					
Obtaining relevant facts				A	S	E	C_6	C_6	6^i	6^i	
Analysis of facts				A	E	C_5					
Review	A	A		E					$4^{i,o}$	$4^{i,o}$	
Formulation				E	C						
Articulation		A	A	A	C_4	S	E		6°	6°	
Training for implementation				E	S	E					
Execution and control	A	A		A	S	E	C_6		6°	6°	

Development of a descriptive model of the system

The third phase of the MIS design process involves the utilization of the user sets and decision areas to develop a descriptive model of the organizational and environmental systems which are relevant to the MIS. This is done in a two-dimensional format which is an adaptation and extension of the concept of a *linear responsibility chart* (LRC).[8] The LRC is a simple organizational model which was originally introduced to provide a more realistic description of the operation of organizations than does the traditional hierarchical organization chart. The method used to accomplish this is to describe authorities, responsibilities, and roles in a matrix form which relates positions and tasks through the use of coded symbols designating the specific roles to be played by each position in the accomplishment of each task.

Table 7-3 shows an LRC which describes the relationships among various *task elements* (listed down the rows of the chart) and various *user groups;* positions and interfacing organizations as listed at the head of the columns.

The entries in Table 7-3 represent a number of organizational characteristics with regard to the single decision area described:

1. authority and responsibility relationships
2. initiation characteristics
3. input-output characteristics

The codes used to describe these characteristics for internal positions are

E-Execution

A-Approval

C-Consultation

S-Supervision

Numbered subscripts on these role descriptors serve to identify the specific relationship.

For instance, the first row of the table tells us that the marketing analyst (7) performs the analysis of routine product complaints, since he is designated as the executor (E). He consults with salespeople in doing this as denoted by C_7. He is supervised (S) by the product manager, and the department manager has responsibility for approving his work (A). The department manager consults with the sales manager in determining this approval (C_4). Also, both the field sales depart-

---

[8] See David I. Cleland and William R. King, *Systems Analysis and Project Management* (New York: McGraw-Hill, 1968), pp. 193, 196–198.

ment provides both input (i) and output (o) to the marketing analyst (7) to permit him to perform this task.

The model depicted in Table 7-3 is an abstract description of the way the system actually operates with regard to the single decision area. While descriptive models such as this are often developed by systems analysts to provide themselves with a basis for understanding the functioning of a system, the purpose for this descriptive model in this methodology is, in fact, prescriptive. However, the use of the model in this fashion first requires that a comparable normative model be developed.

Development of a normative model of the system

The descriptive model of the organizational and environmental system provided by Table 7-3 and other such charts is a useful road map for guiding informational analysis. It provides insights into who actually does what, the interactions among organizational units and between internal and external units, the general nature of information required, the direction of information flow, and the manner in which information requirements are generated.

However, the use of a model of this variety as the sole basis for the design of information systems would represent an abrogation of the information analyst's proper role. Rather than creating an information system to serve an existing organizational system, he should attempt to influence the restructuring of the decision-making process so that the MMIS may be oriented toward the support of a more nearly optimal process.

To do this, the analyst may call on the best knowledge and theory of marketing management to construct a normative model of the organization which is consistent with, and comparable to, the descriptive one previously developed.

A normative model looks much like the descriptive model of Table 7-3 except that it will normally involve more entries. This is so because the normative model is an exercise in *idealized system design,* which will normally reflect many activities that the organization *should* be performing that are not depicted in the descriptive model. [9]

However, it is just as inappropriate for the analyst to impose his concept of the way the organization and its MMIS should operate as it is to slavishly design the MMIS to conform to the way in which the organization does operate. To meet the criterion of broad optimality based on improved effectiveness and usability, the designer must seek some consensus model which can serve as a realistic basis for system design.

[9] See R. L. Ackoff, *A Concept of Corporate Planning* (New York: Wiley, 1971).

Development of a consensus model of the system

Although few organizations desiring an MMIS would be willing to restructure their organization's authority and responsibility patterns and relationships to suit the needs of the MMIS, it is generally recognized that procedural improvement is a valid by-product of MMIS design. Therefore, organizations are normally willing to consider some elements of a normative organizational model rather than to insist simply that the MMIS solely service existing procedures, functions, and authorities.

The development of a *consensus model* hinges on an objective comparison of a descriptive model such as that of Table 7-3 with a comparable normative model. This comparison and evaluation must be done by managers with the aid and advice of analysts.

One possible medium for this process is that of a participative executive development program. The program involves the MMIS users as ''students'' and the MMIS analysts as ''teachers.'' The normative model is developed and discussed in lecture and discussion sessions. After it has been communicated fully, workshops may be used to facilitate the detailed evaluation and comparison of the descriptive and normative models. Recommendations emanating from the workshops may then be reviewed by top management, and those which were approved can be incorporated into a consensus model of the system.

Thus, the consensus model looks like the LRC in Table 7-3. However, if it is developed as an organizational consensus of, ''how we want the organization to operate,'' it can form the basis for an MMIS. Since a consensus model emanates from a comparison of a descriptive model (''how we operate now'') with a normative model (''how we theoretically should operate''), it integrates the best of current practice with those aspects of theory which are considered by the organization's managers to have practical applicability.

An LRC consensus model of the organization in terms of tasks, roles and responsibilities of user groups, information to be processed, etc., can form the basis for an MMIS design. As we indicate in the next chapter, it is a road map of the organization which can be used to analyze specific information requirements and flows.

Summary

The general design of MMIS begins with the establishment of system objectives. If this is done well, it is done within a broad framework of strategic systems planning, which emphasizes the identification of underlying problems and opportunities, rather than within narrower frameworks of correcting organizational ills and remedying information deficiencies.

The operationalization of this approach to the strategic systems planning approach involves:

1. Defining the organization in systems terms which emphasize organizational claimants and the nature of their claims
2. Delineating objectives for each claimant group
3. Identifying organizational objectives
4. Developing system objectives based on claimant and organizational objectives

These system objectives must be supplemented with the specification of system constraints. Such constraints may be translated into desirable or attainable MMIS characteristics. For instance, organizational policies may both constrain and offer opportunities for the MMIS. Personnel capabilities may constrain the nature of the system which can be developed and, inevitably, so will cost constraints.

Based on these objectives and constraints, the MMIS general design may be specified through the use of a linear responsibility chart model. Such a model describes the organization to be supported by the MMIS in terms of tasks to be supported, user groups, interfacing environmental organizations, authorities, responsibilities, and information flow patterns.

A descriptive LRC model can be developed to show how the organization currently operates. This, together with a comparable normative model showing how analysts believe that it should operate, can be used to generate a third model, a consensus model, which reflects how the organization itself chooses to operate and to be supported by the MMIS. This consensus model is the MMIS general design or road map which guides the development of the detailed MMIS design.

EXERCISES

1. What is wrong with using organizational problem areas as a guide to the systems which need to be developed to improve organizational performance?
2. Why are symptoms often viewed as problems in organizations? Is there a danger of this happening with the medical symptoms exhibited by an individual as well? Give an example.
3. What is the difference between systems problem solving and strategic systems planning? Relate this difference to the requirements which might be placed on an MMIS in organizations which practice each variety of problem solving.
4. Table 7-1 provides an excellent checklist for use in considering the impact of any contemplated action. Can you show how it might be so used?

5. Refute the following statement or substantiate it by an example of why all stockholders might not have claims of the same nature: All stockholders are not the same and, therefore, the treatment of their claims in Table 7-1 is inadequate.

6. How does the idea of integrating management systems fit with the principle of modular MMIS design as expounded in Chapter 6?

7. Figure 7-2 shows the relationships among clientele objectives, organizational objectives, and system objectives. Give other examples and show how an objective of the general public, say cleaner air, could be incorporated into the other two levels of objectives.

8. Why is it important to identify system constraints early in the general design phase? After all, wouldn't it be better to think big and not worry about constraints until later?

9. Describe precisely the role played by the existing system in the MMIS general design process described in the chapter.

10. Relate the general design process to each of the principles in Chapter 6 and evaluate how well it implements each principle.

11. Why not just design the MMIS on the basis of the normative LRC model? After all, isn't this the model that describes the best way for the organization to operate?

REFERENCES

Ackoff, R. L. *A Concept of Corporate Planning*. New York: Wiley, 1970.

Ashenhurst, R. L., ed. "Curriculum Recommendations for Graduate Professional Programs in Information Systems: A Report of the ACM Curriculum Committee on Computer Education for Management." *Communications of the ACM* 15 (May 1972): 363–398.

Churchman, C. W.; Ackoff, R. L.; and Arnoff, E. L. *Introduction to Operations Research*. New York: Wiley, 1957.

——— and Schainblatt, A. H. "The Researcher and the Manager: A Dialectic of Implementation." *Management Science* II (February 1965): B69–B87.

Cleland, David I., and King, William R. *Systems Analysis and Project Management*, 2d ed., New York: McGraw-Hill, 1975.

Davis, G. B. *Management Information Systems: Conceptual Foundations, Structure and Development*. New York: McGraw-Hill, 1974.

Diebold, J. "Bad Decisions on Computer Use." *Harvard Business Review*, January–February 1969.

Eilon, S. "How Scientific is OR?" *OMEGA* 3 (1975): 1–8.

Huysmans, J. H. B. M. *The Implementation of Operations Research: An Approach to the Joint Consideration of Social and Technological Aspects*. New York: Wiley, 1970.

King, William R. "Methodological Optimality in Operations Research." *OMEGA*, February 1976.

——— and Cleland, David I. "The Design of Management Information Systems: An Information Analysis Approach." *Management Science*, November 1975.

————. "Manager Analyst Teamwork in Management Information Systems." *Business Horizons,* April 1971.

McKinsey and Co. "Unlocking the Computer's Profit Potential." *Computers and Automation,* April 1969.

Murdick, R. G. "MIS Development Procedures." *Journal of Systems Management.* December 1970, pp. 22–26.

———— and Ross, J. E. *Information Systems for Modern Management,* 2d ed. Englewood Cliffs, N.J.: Prentice-Hall, 1975.

8

Development of the Detailed
Design of the System

O nce the general design of the system has been developed and approved by top management, detailed design activity may begin. The detailed design consists of system specifications, flowcharts, equipment and personnel specifications, procedures, file designs, hardware specifications, and an implementation plan.

In this chapter, we focus primarily on the translation of the general design into this level of detail, and do not go into the many esoteric areas such as data structures, operating systems, and computer languages which are a necessary prerequisite to the specification of a detailed design. Here, our emphasis is on the managerial aspects of detailed design rather than on the computer aspects, which are more properly treated in a computer science text.

A grid such as that in Table 8-1 provides the best overall understanding of the design details. The figure shows one-half of the grid crossed out because it is redundant with the lower half. The lower half shows various pair-wise relationships between the elements comprising the grid—objectives, decisions, positions, reports, and information elements.

The pair-wise specification of these elements represents a useful device for understanding the general system design and for translating it into a detailed design.

For instance, consider element 1 in Table 8-1, the element which represents the relationship between the objectives and the decisions and activities. To fill in this element of the table requires that each objective be identified and that each decision and activity that the system is to support be related to each objective.

Table 8-2 represents an explanation of part of element 1 of Table 8-1. It shows a breakdown oriented toward decisions and activities in which the various objectives to which each decision or activity is addressed are enumerated. For instance, the decision on the choice of a vendor has impact on five different objectives, from cost reduction to the maintenance of good relations with vendors who are also customers.

TABLE 8-1 System Design Grid

	Objectives	Decisions and Activities	Positions	Reports	Information Elements
Objectives					
Decisions and Activities	(1)				
Positions	(2)	(3)			
Reports	(4)	(5)	(6)		
Information elements	(7)	(8)	(9)	(10)	

TABLE 8-2 Portion of Element 1 from Table 8-1

Decision or Activity	Objectives
Determine economical order quantity	Cost reduction
	Management effectiveness
	Achievement of volume discounts
Monitor supplier performance	Cost reduction
	Maintenance of multiple supply sources
Choose vendor for order	Cost reduction
	Maintenance of multiple supply sources
	Achievement of volume discounts
	Achievement of timely deliveries
	Maintaining good relations with vendors who are also customers

A similar objectives-oriented table could be developed in which each objective is listed, and all of the decisions and activities which relate to it are pulled together in one place.

Each of the other numbered elements of Table 8-1 can also be so represented. At the lower levels of Table 8-1, one is getting into the detailed design of the system. For instance, element 10 in Table 8-1 involves those information elements which are to be contained in reports, as illustrated in Table 8-3.

While elements comprising certain elements in Table 8-1 are of obvious necessity, in that they identify the detailed design of the system (such as the report-information element of Table 8-3), others are of use primarily because they provide a check on the validity of the system design. *An explication of all these relationships serves to make sure that information is being incorporated into the system for a specific purpose*—not just because it appears to be useful. Table 8-1, taken in its entirety, specifies the various relationships which must be dealt with in developing the general design and in translating it into a detailed design of the system. It can be used as a guide to system development and as a checklist against which a preliminary design of the system can be evaluated for comprehensiveness and content.

Relating Decisions and Information

The relationship between decisions (and activities) and information has been put forth in previous chapters as a basic linkage which can be made use of in MMIS design.

The linkage between the decisions and activities in which the organization

TABLE 8-3

Report	Information Element
Buyer price analysis report	Item code
	Part number
	Supplier
	Unit cost for the base period
	Unit cost for the current month
	Total quantity for the base period
	Total quantity for the current month
Vendor delivery report	Buyer code
	Vendor name
	Vendor number
	Total order value last year
	Number of orders last year
	Open orders
	Total value of open orders
	Number of orders behind schedule
	Value of orders behind schedule
	Percentage of total number behind schedule
	Percentage of total value behind schedule

engages and the *information requirements* which emanate from those decisions and activities is the heart of detailed design of the MMIS. Thus, element 8 in Table 8-1 is a critical part of the overall conceptual framework for an MMIS.

The general design of the MMIS, in the form of the consensus organizational model of Chapter 7, specifies a variety of decisions and activities by activity descriptions such as initiate, execute, approve, etc. These represent the decisions and activities which are to be supported by the MMIS. Since this support is to be in the form of information, it is necessary that the information required for each decision or activity be delineated.

Information requirements

We have dealt with various concepts of the need for information in previous chapters, and we have also made note of the inadequacy of an MMIS design procedure which is based on asking managers to state their information needs. Such specifications of requirements are invariably overstated. It is not this result that is so bad in itself, but rather the actions often taken by system designers faced with resolving the dilemma of huge requirements and limited resources.

As pointed out in the Enthoven "homey example" in Chapter 7, this situation is often resolved by an arbitrary cutting back of the information requirements that managers have stated. This cutback process is often ill-informed, because it must, of necessity, be performed by analysts. The managers have, after all, already stated their requirements, and they cannot admit to having overstated them by voluntarily cutting them back! Such arbitrary cutbacks often ignore the underlying purpose for which information is needed as well as the interdependencies among various information items; for example, the fact that one item of the data may not be useful unless another item is also available.

In such a situation, one manager, who had stated that the Standard Industrial Classification (SIC) code designator was required for each customer, was forced to get along with a three-digit SIC number rather than a five-digit one after some arbitrary approaches were applied to resolving the ''requirements versus dollars'' dilemma.[1] Unfortunately, the three-digit code was entirely useless to him, but he found that he could do nothing to influence the arbitrary decision which had been made to ensure ''fair'' treatment to all of those managers who had to have their information requirements cut back.

Using decision models to determine information requirements [2]

The various ways in which decision models may be used to specify information requirements were discussed in Chapter 3. Models may be made use of in the MMIS design process because *each of the elements in the consensus model of the general system* (as described in Chapter 7) *is a decision or activity which may be modeled.*

Managers and analysts can work together to explicate these decision and activity models, as specified in the consensus LRC general design, even if some are of the mental model variety.

Indeed, most of the models actually used for decision making in an organization are implicit rather than explicit. Most large organizations have formalized and computerized models for operational control. Inventory reports, production schedules, cost analyses, and the like are prepared using simple formalized models. However, the way in which these simple models and data are synthesized in the important decision-making models of the organization is usually imprecisely defined. Most of these strategic models are buried in the minds of the managers who make these high-level decisions.

---

[1] The SIC code system describes firms in terms of broad industrial categories and successively finer subcategories, through the use of a numerical designator. A code number with a larger number of digits more finely defines a firm's particular industrial subcategory.

[2] Portions of this section are adapted with permission from the author's paper with David I. Cleland, ''The Design of Management Information Systems: An Information Analysis Approach,'' *Management Science,* November 1975.

The effective use of models in MMIS design revolves around an interactive process between managers and analysts which has a goal of model explication or verbalization. If the manager's mental models can at least be verbalized, they can be used in the MMIS design process to define information requirements. They need not be reduced to mathematical form or be made completely explicit to be used in this way, so long as they can be communicated.

For a demonstration of how this can be done, consider the various code descriptions of activities and decisions in the LRC systems model as described in Chapter 7:

E—Execution

A—Approval

C—Consultation

S—Supervision

Now, consider how the models underlying each of these activities may be explicated through a process of manager-analyst interaction. For instance, an approval activity can be detailed in terms of the criteria applied to the approval decision, and each execution activity will need to have a model of the execution activity specified.

The term *model* as used in this context is a broad interpretation of the usual usage. It includes not only sophisticated mathematical models, but also simple descriptive models and even the mental models which are a part of every decision-making process. Such models are difficult to assess in objective terms, but the necessity for doing so in MIS design has become clear.

To illustrate how such a mental model can be specified, consider a hypothetical portion of a discussion between a manager who makes hiring decisions and an analyst who is trying to help him formulate his decision model objectively.

Analyst: What is the most important factor that you use to select the best man for the job?

Manager: His aptitude test scores. It is critical that we get someone with the aptitude for the job.

Analyst: Is that all that you need?

Manager: Oh no, job experience is important too.

Analyst: What if you had a man with high aptitude scores, but no experience and another with experience and modest scores; which would you choose?

Manager: The experienced one, if we had good evidence that his experience had been meaningful and that he had really performed well.

The discussion would continue much beyond this, but this brief portion demonstrates how a mental model can be made objective. In three questions, the analyst has begun to construct a model which relates job success to two predictor elements—aptitude and experience. Further, he has begun (through the third question) to get some rough "priority weights" among the predictor elements.

In some decision areas, the end product of such a discussion might well be an objective model such as

$$y = a_1 x_1 + a_2 x_2 + a_3 x_3 + \ldots + a_n x_n + b$$

where y is an indicator of job success, such as a performance rating; the x's are predictors such as aptitude test scores and years of experience; and the a's are relative importance weights determined subjectively by the manager. Of course, in many areas, no model as specific as this one will be feasible. The remainder of the process to be described recognizes this, and allows for both formal and informal decision models.

The final step in the process is the determination of information requirements based on the consensus model of the system and on the particular decision models which have been explicated for each of the entries in the chart representing the consensus model. These decision models serve to specify particular information requirements; and the consensus model of the system prescribes the linkages and relationships of these elements of information.

If, for example, an approval activity is indicated in the consensus model, it should be detailed in terms of the specific factors and criteria which need to be considered in determining whether approval is to be given; for example, the specific levels of these factors which need to be achieved for approval to be granted.

To illustrate, suppose that an approval activity associated with a hiring decision is under examination. The manager might have explained his model for the approval activity as follows:

1. First, check to see that all company hiring policies have been followed.
2. Then, check to see that no one already in the organization desires to fill the job.
3. Then, check to see if the candidate helps us fulfill our objectives with regard to minority group hiring, and, if not, make sure no equally good candidates are available who will help us fulfill them.

These criteria specify a rather specific set of information requirements:

1. Hiring policies
2. Data on candidate and hiring procedure relevant to each hiring policy
3. Comparable data on existing personnel
4. Data on job transfer desires of existing personnel
5. Minority group status of candidate
6. Data on other candidates

Of course, in order that they represent operational information requirements, these elements would need to be detailed much further. However, once specifications such as these have been made, the process of further detailing them is a straightforward one.

Alternately, suppose that an execution activity has been explicated in the form of the formal model of the equation given above. Such a model specifies information requirements in a number of ways. First, the performance measure, y, represents an information element which must be provided by the MIS. Although such data will not be available for candidates, historical data will be necessary to judge the validity of the model as it continues to be used. Secondly, the predictor variables (the x's) are input data for the decision, as are the weights (the a's).

Thus, such a model would provide a list of information requirements of the following form:

1. Historical data on performance ratings of personnel
2. Applicant's aptitude-test score's
3. Applicant's experience in years
4. Minority-group membership
5. Relative-importance weight for aptitude-test score
6. Relative-importance weight for experience

.

.

.

etc.

If more sophisticated models are developed, other information requirements may also be determined. For instance, the solution to an optimization model may itself entail information specifications, as noted in Chapter 3.

The operational manager-analyst design process

The concept of manager-analyst cooperative system design is not new. However, if this cooperation is to be raised above the level of maintaining contact or infrequent interaction, the concept must be operationalized. This may be done by defining the process more precisely and by assigning responsibilities for the various phases of the model-based MIS design process.

Figure 8-1 is a model of an MIS design process which attempts to provide a basis for manager-analyst shared and interrelated responsibilities.[3] In the figure, each activity is designated as the prime responsibility of the manager (M) or the analyst (A) or as shared (M, A). In the upper left, the manager and analyst are

[3] Adapted with permission from William R. King, and David I. Cleland, "Manager-Analyst Teamwork in MIS," *Business Horizons,* April 1971.

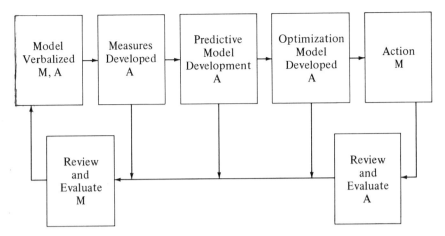

FIGURE 8-1 **MIS design process**

shown working together to verbalize the model of the choice, approval, supervisory role, or whatever activity is being dealt with. Then the analyst is given the
task of finding measures for the factors which have been enunciated. The entire
process is a series of feed-back loops, since the analyst must return to the manager for review and evaluation of his work at the completion of each of the three
tasks assigned primarily to him. In each loop, the manager and analyst also
jointly consider revision of previous steps.

If the two agree on the model's general form and the measures to be used,
the analyst tries to construct explicit predictive or optimization models which can
be used in the situation. For instance, in a market selection problem like that discussed in Chapter 3, the analyst first developed regression predictive models and,
finally, a discriminant cost optimization model. Of course, in many instances it is
impossible to develop adequate predictive models, in which case the process simply continues on to the right.

Once some informal, predictive, or optimization model is agreed on, the
manager decides and takes some action. The analyst is then given an opportunity
to review and evaluate the results. Together, they then determine whether a
complete rerun of the process is necessary.

The model that is finally developed determines the information requirements
for this particular decision problem or area in the organization through its predictive variables, criterion, solution, and sensitivity information. This relationship
between models and information requirements is that which was specified in
Chapter 3. The analyst then goes on to another activity as indicated in the consensus LRC model, and the manager is left to perform the activity. Hopefully, he
has both a better understanding of his activity and will be provided with adequate
information to solve it.

This process of creating the MMIS is as important as the end product. The model-based design process is one that emphasizes both the design process and the product; too many other approaches to design focus almost exclusively on the end product. The model-based process is most likely to provide the manager with the right information on an economical basis. Also, however, it virtually ensures that he will come to a better understanding of his job and the decisions which it entails. If the model-based design leads solely to better decisions through better understanding, rather than through better information, it more than justifies itself.

In most instances, the loss is substantial if the system is inadequate or obsolete by the time it is implemented. With the model-based MIS design process, even if such a "failure" were to occur, much of the real value of the design process has already been achieved.

Completion of the Detailed MMIS Design

The detailed design process just described creates explicit relations between the organization's structure, its objectives, and the information that the MMIS is to incorporate into its data base. Once this process has been completed, a number of other steps must be taken before the detailed design is complete:

1. Subsystem definition
2. Graphical systems design
3. Data base specification
4. Software specification
5. Hardware specification
6. Development of an implementation plan
7. Documentation of the design

Subsystem definition

Although the MMIS subsystems will be defined in general terms at the general design stage, the general design process and the determination of information requirements may lead to revisions in the desired subsystems. In any case, it will be necessary at the detailed design stage to specify how each activity, as specified in a consensus LRC model like Table 7-2, will be grouped with other activities to form subsystems and to specify the inputs and outputs of each activity.

Graphical systems design

However scientific the MMIS design process may be purported by some to be, it inevitably comes to a point, very much like that in all of engineering design, where an analyst sits down with the wealth of data and subsystem definitions and

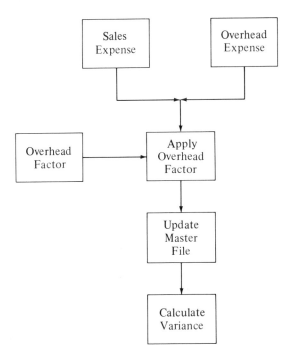

FIGURE 8-2 Task-oriented flowchart

proceeds to portray graphically the logical system and subsystem relationships. This is usually done in the form of flowcharts which will subsequently form the basis for software development.

Two varieties of flowcharts are commonly used—those which show *relationships among tasks* and those that are *forms oriented*. A simplified portion of a task-oriented chart is shown as Figure 8-2. The forms-oriented chart of Figure 8-3 identifies all forms which are to be used and traces the flow of each copy through the organization.

Integrated Processing. Economics can be achieved in systems design through the use of common modules and integrated processing. At this point in the design process, such considerations come into play.

Integrated processing is achieved by designing related activities into a single subsystem in order to simplify the overall system and reduce redundancies. Davis gives an example of an order entry system in which the recording of an order is designed to initiate a processing sequence in which each step uses new data as well as data from prior processing.[4] The steps in the sequence are shown in Table 8-4.

[4] G. B. Davis, *Management Information Systems: Conceptual Foundations, Structure, and Development* (New York: McGraw-Hill, 1974).

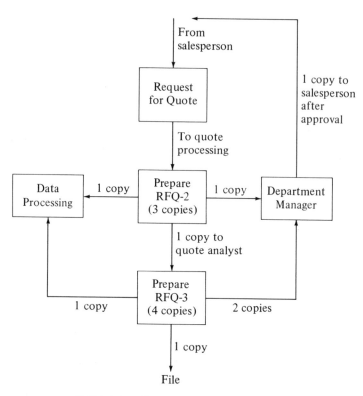

FIGURE 8-3 Form-oriented flowchart

Data base specification

Although all of the information requirements have been previously spelled out in extensive form, the detailed design of the data base in terms of various master files and their relationships must be done in much the same fashion as for subsystems.

This is an activity of detailed design which requires that each element of data be specified in terms of its source, length, form, update frequency, retention, and end use. When all of these data about data have been compiled, they are grouped by subsystem, checked for redundancies and omissions and organized into a data base consisting of files; for example, for open order, customers, products, and vendors.

Software Specifications

Software, or programs, are developed on the basis of *program flowcharts* which show logical relationships and sequences of steps to be executed by the computer. When such flowcharts are put into *coded* form, that is, into the form of de-

TABLE 8-4 Order Entry System *

Step	New Data Entered	Documents Produced
Order entry	Sales representative identification Customer identification Items ordered Quantity of each item	Order acknowledgment Credit exception notice Order register Picking document Items out of stock Items to be ordered
Shipping	Actual quantity shipped	Shipping document
Invoicing	Freight cost	Invoice register Sales journal Back-order register
Collection	Amounts received Returns and allowances	Statements Credit memos Returns and allowances register Cash receipts journal Accounts receivable Aging
Analysis		Sales by sales representative, district, customer, or other category

* Adapted with permission from G. B. Davis, *Management Information Systems: Conceptual Foundations, Structure, and Development* (New York: McGraw-Hill, 1974), pp. 222–223.

tailed instructions which can be input directly to the computer, and tested and documented, they form the basic knowledge which the system possesses and the basis for man-machine communications.

Hardware Specifications

At some earlier stage in the process, the designers will begin developing specifications in terms of the volume of data to be processed, the speed and accuracy required, and the nature of the required hardware system. At the stage of detailed design, these specifications must be put into detailed form to permit the assessment of varieties of commercially available hardware in terms of their cost and performance capabilities.

Implementation Plan

Despite the fact that the entire systems design process is created around a framework of ensuring the acceptability of the system, it is desirable to develop an implementation plan. Such a plan designates who will give presentations describing the system, when and to whom, what documents will be prepared, schedules for demonstrations, etc.

An important part of such a plan is a description of the system which includes a specification of the roles to be played by various people—managers, system consultants, operators, etc.—in the day-to-day use of the system.

Documentation of the Design

The output of a detailed design phase is a set of documents which describe the system, its operation, and its justification for existence. In effect, such a document is a very detailed explosion of the proposal which will have been prepared at a much earlier stage in the design process (discussed in Chapter 9).

Summary

Detailed MMIS designs reflect specific reports and the items of information contained in each, flows of information, frequency of flows, and the organizational positions to be supplied with various reports.

The conceptual framework which relates the general design to this detailed MMIS design can be developed in terms of a hierarchy of relationships among (1) objectives, (2) decisions and activities, (3) positions, (4) reports, and (5) information elements.

An MMIS design should permit a complete explication of the content and structure of the MMIS with respect to every pair of these elements. For instance, each *report* is made up of *information elements;* each *report* is provided to persons holding *positions* in the organization; and each *information element* should be incorporated into the system because it is related to specific *decisions and activities.*

The essence of developing a detailed systems design from the general design is the development of the *information requirements* which are inherent in the decisions and activities as specified in the general design. Whether these decisions and activities involve formal or informal processes, they may be explicated in order to assess the information which is required to support each. This explication may be accomplished through a process of manager-analyst interaction.

Once the data base for the MMIS has been defined in extensive form, including all information necessary to support each organizational decision and activity, the detailed MMIS design may be completed. This involves the refined specification of subsystems, graphical design, data base design; software and hardware specification; the development of an implementation plan; and the documentation of the finalized design.

EXERCISES

1. Select one of the numbered elements of Table 8-1 that has not been illustrated in detail in the text and give a detailed illustration of that element for a particular MMIS subsystem.

2. How does element 3 in Table 8-1 relate to the LRC model in Chapter 7?

3. How does element 6 in Table 8-1 relate to the flowchart of Figure 8-3?

4. Element 5 in Table 8-1 relates reports to decisions and activities. The use of element 6, which relates reports to positions, is rather clear since it shows who gets which reports, but what use can be made of a detailed specification of an element such as 5?

5. Suppose that a 20 percent cut is ordered in the budget for the data base and that this results in a 20 percent across the board cut in the information requirements which have been proposed by various managers. What is the inevitable result of such a cut?

6. Try to explicate the mental model that you use in purchasing a car in the terms described in this chapter.

7. Can you think of an area of your life in which the mental model that you use to make decisions is one that can easily be quantified (written down in algebraic form such as: if $x > y$, do z, and if not, do q)?

8. Try to develop a simple system design which incorporates both the competition subsystem and the intelligence subsystem as described in Chapter 5. Illustrate the subsystem relationships in terms of data flows, etc., in an attempt to integrate the two subsystems into something that is more than just two independent subsystems. Use a graphical approach.

9. Develop a simple forms-oriented design for an intelligence subsystem that involves:
   a. Visitation reports from salespeople and managers who visit the same customers
   b. Questions posed by managers to be answered, if possible, by salespeople who are in daily contact with the competitor's salespeople

10. Construct a detailed implementation plan for an intelligence subsystem of an MMIS. Be sure to consider the psychology of people who may be "turned off" by such an idea as well as the need for involving many people in such a system as "intelligence agents."

REFERENCES

Blumenthal, S. C. *Management Information Systems.* Englewood Cliffs, N.J.: Prentice-Hall, 1969.

Couger, J. D. and Knapp, R. W., eds., *Systems Analysis Techniques.* New York: Wiley, 1973.

Davis, G. B. *Management Information Systems: Conceptual Foundations, Structure, and Development.* New York: McGraw-Hill, 1974.

IBM. "Study Organization Plan: Documentation Techniques." IBM Manual FC20-8075-0 (1960–1961).

Lynch, H. J. "ADS: A Technique in System Documentation." *Database,* Spring 1969.

Morgan, R. G. and Soden, J. V., "Understanding MIS Failures." *DATA Base,* Winter 1973, pp. 157–171.

Murdick, R. G., and Ross, J. E. *Information Systems for Modern Management,* 2d ed. Englewood Cliffs, N.J.: Prentice-Hall, 1975.

Nolan, R. L. "Managing the Computer Resource: A Stage Hypothesis." *Communications of the ACM,* July 1973, pp. 399–405.

Teichroew, D., and Sayani, H. "Automation of System Building." *Datamation,* 15 August 1971.

9

Planning and Managing the MMIS Development Project

I In Chapter 7, we noted that the first phase of MMIS development involves planning for the development project. However, we deferred discussion of it to treat the two phases which are the central core of the effort, the general and detailed design phases.

Now, we return to consideration of the phase involving planning for the project. In this chapter, we consider the broad range of activities stretching from the initial conception of the project, through development, implementation, operation and eventually divestment—the point at which the decision is made to replace the MMIS.

System Life Cycles

The concept of a *system life cycle* is critical to an understanding of the management tasks and processes involved in MMIS development. The U.S. Department of Defense and the National Aeronautics and Space Administration have extensively defined and detailed phases which should be encountered with hardware systems development. Their concept of the life cycle in the development of a system recognizes a natural order of thought and action which is pervasive in the development of many kinds of systems, be they for commercial products, space exploration, or management.

In each phase of this system life cycle, different levels and varieties of specific thought and action are required within the organization to perform the necessary functions and to assess the efficacy of the system. The phases of this cycle serve to illustrate the concept of a life cycle and its importance in the development of a system.

Taken together, Tables 9-1 through 9-5 provide a detailed outline of the overall life cycle of the development of a system. Of course, the terminology used in these tables is not applicable to every system which might be under development, since the terminology generally applied to the development of an MMIS is often different from that applied to weapons systems. However, whatever terminology is used, the concepts are applicable to all such complex systems.

The Conceptual Phase

The germ of the idea for a system may evolve from current organizational problems or from a perception that opportunities are not being identified and used to advantage. The conceptual phase is one in which the idea is conceived and given preliminary evaluation.

During the conceptual phase, the organizational environment is examined, needs are assessed, preliminary system objectives and alternatives are evaluated,

TABLE 9-1 Conceptual Phase *

1. Determine existing needs or potential deficiencies of existing systems.
2. Establish system concepts which provide initial strategic guidance to overcome existing or potential deficiencies.
3. Determine initial technical, environmental, and economic feasibility and practicability of the system.
4. Examine alternative ways of accomplishing the system objectives.
5. Provide initial estimates:
   a. What will the system cost?
   b. When will the system be available?
   c. What will the system do?
   d. How will the system be integrated into existing systems?
6. Identify the human and nonhuman resources required to support the system.
7. Select preliminary system designs which will satisfy the system objectives.
8. Determine preliminary system interfaces.
9. Establish a system organization.

* Tables 9-1 through 9-5 are adapted with permission from the author's text with David I. Cleland, *Systems Analysis and Project Management,* 2d ed. (New York: McGraw-Hill, 1975).

and the first examination is performed of the performance, cost, and time aspects of the system's development. It is also during this phase that basic development strategy, organization, and resource requirements are conceived. The fundamental purpose of the conceptual phase is to conduct a white-paper study of the requirements in order to provide a basis for further detailed evaluation. Table 9-1 shows the details of these efforts.

There will typically be a high mortality rate of potential system concepts during the conceptual phase of the life cycle. Rightly so, since the study process conducted during this phase should identify those systems that have high risk and are technically, environmentally, or economically infeasible or impractical.

The Definition Phase

The fundamental purpose of the definition phase is to determine, as soon as possible and as accurately as possible, the cost, schedule, performance, and resource requirements and whether all elements, projects, and subsystems will fit together economically and technically.

The definition phase simply tells in more detail what it is we want to do, when we want to do it, how we will accomplish it, and what it will cost. The definition phase allows the organization to conceive and define the system fully before it starts to put the system into its environment physically. Simply stated, the definition phase dictates that one stop and take time to look around to see if

TABLE 9-2 Definition Phase

1. Firm identification of the human and nonhuman resources required
2. Preparation of final system performance requirements
3. Preparation of detailed plans required to support the system
4. Determination of realistic cost, schedule, and performance requirements
5. Identification of areas of the system where high risk and uncertainty exist, and delineation of plans for further exploration of these areas
6. Definition of intersystem and intrasystem interfaces
7. Determination of necessary support subsystems
8. Identification and initial preparation of the documentation required to support the system, such as operating manuals.

the particular system is what is really wanted before the resources are committed to putting it into operation and production. If the system concept has survived through the end of the conceptual phase, a conditional approval for further study and development is given. The definition phase provides opportunities to review and confirm the decision to continue development, to begin a system module, and to make a production or installation decision.

Decisions that are made during and at the end of the definition phase might very well be decisions to cancel further work on the system and redirect organizational resources elsewhere. The elements of this phase are described in Table 9-2.

Acquisition Phase

The purpose of the acquisition phase is to acquire and test the system elements and the total system itself using the standards developed during the preceding phases. The acquisition process involves such things as the actual setting up of the system, the installation of hardware, the allocation of authority and responsibility, the construction of facilities, and the finalization of supporting documentation. Table 9-3 details this phase.

The Operational Phase

The fundamental role of the manager of a system during the operational phase is to provide the resource support required to accomplish system objectives. This phase indicates that the system has been proven economical, feasible, and practicable and that it will be used to accomplish the desired ends for which it has been developed. In this phase the manager's functions change somewhat. He is

TABLE 9-3 Acquisition Phase

1. Updating of detailed plans conceived and defined during the preceding phases
2. Identification and management of the resources required to facilitate the production processes such as inventory, supplies, labor, funds, etc.
3. Verification of system production specifications
4. Beginning of production, construction, and installation
5. Final preparation and dissemination of policy and procedural documents
6. Performance of final testing to determine adequacy of the system to do the things it is intended to do
7. Development of technical manuals and affiliated documentation describing how the system is intended to operate
8. Development of plans to support the system during its operational phase

less concerned with planning and organizing and more concerned with controlling the system's operation along the predetermined lines of performance. His responsibilities for planning and organization are not entirely neglected—there are always elements of these functions remaining—but he places more emphasis on motivating the human element of the system and controlling the utilization of resources of the total system. It is during this phase that the system may lose its identity per se and be assimilated into the institutional framework of the organization. Table 9-4 shows the important elements of this phase.

The Divestment Phase

The divestment phase is the one in which the organization gets out of the "business" it began with the conceptual phase. Every system—be it a product system, a weapons system, a management information system, or whatever—has a finite lifetime. Too often this goes unrecognized, with the result that outdated and unprofitable products are retained, inefficient management systems are used, or inadequate equipment and facilities are tolerated. Only by the specific and con-

TABLE 9-4 Operational Phase

1. Use of the system by the intended user or customer
2. Actual integration of the system into existing organizational systems
3. Evaluation of the technical, social, and economic sufficiency of the project to meet actual operating conditions
4. Provision of feedback to organizational planners concerned with developing new projects and systems
5. Evaluation of the adequacy of supporting systems

TABLE 9-5 Divestment Phase

1. System phasedown
2. Development of plans transferring responsibility to supporting organizations
3. Divestment or transfer of resources to other systems
4. Development of "lessons learned from system" for inclusion in qualitative-quantitative data base to include:
   a. Assessment of system by users
   b. Major problems encountered and their solution
   c. Technological advances
   d. Advancements in knowledge relative to strategic objectives
   e. New or improved management techniques
   f. Recommendations for future research and development
   g. Recommendations for the management of future systems
   h. Other major lessons learned during the course of the system

tinuous consideration of the divestment possibilities can the organization realistically hope to avoid these contingencies. Table 9-5 relates to the divestment phase.

Of course, if the system has been designed from the evolutionary point of view described in Chapter 6, it should, theoretically, never require divestment. However, this theoretical standard is difficult to achieve, and most future systems, like all past systems, will probably reach a point of diminishing returns where they are best scrapped and the job undertaken anew. The critical point in the past has been that some firms have failed to recognize this fact and have stayed with existing systems to a point approaching catastrophe.

Implications of the Project Life Cycle

The project life cycle importantly affects the way in which MMIS development projects may be effectively planned and managed.

The most direct implication involves the recognition that *different skills and resources will be required during the various stages of the life cycle.* For instance, creative design skills are needed in large quantities in the early stages, but not so much in the later stages. Hard-nosed economic analysis skills are needed in the conceptual and definition phases and then again in the divestment phase, but not so much in the other phases. Programmers are needed only for consultative input in the earliest stages, but they become of great importance in the acquisition phase.

The degree of user involvement will also vary greatly throughout the life cycle. User-managers are required on a substantial basis in the early planning stages for determining the firm's needs and the objectives which should be established for the MMIS. They are, as well, an intrinsic part of the user-oriented design process described in Chapters 7 and 8.

The user plays only a consultative role, answering questions and giving interpretations to the programmers and analysts, when the system is actually being installed. In later stages, when the system is in operation, the user again becomes an important system element.

The level of expenditure on the project will also vary greatly during its life cycle, from a modest level in the early *thinking* stages to successively higher levels and then again to lower levels in the later stages. So too with virtually every other measure that one could apply to an MMIS development project, whether the measure be of the input or of the output variety—that is, whether it measures the amount and nature of resources consumed at each stage, or the amount and nature of the benefits produced. The project life cycle necessarily leads to dynamic project characteristics.

Critical Dimensions of the Project

By viewing project life cycles in terms of the measures which may be applied at the various stages of evolution, one is naturally led to question whether there are not a number of universal measures which can be applied to projects, regardless of their nature or specific context.

Three critical general dimensions which can be used for assessing the progress of most projects are *cost, time,* and *performance.* Cost refers to the resources being expended, assessed sometimes in terms of an expenditure rate (e.g., dollars per month), sometimes in terms of total cumulative expenditures, and sometimes in terms of both. Time refers to the timeliness of progress in terms of a schedule which has been set up. Answers to such questions as ''Is the project on schedule?'' ''How many days must be made up?'' etc., reflect this dimension of progress.

The third dimension of project is performance; that is, how is the project meeting its objectives or specifications? The performance of the MMIS may be indicated by the ability of the system under development to meet its objectives. Will the system being designed be able to do the things for which it was intended? Will it be possible to capture various elements of data and to process them in time for the desired end-of-week reports? Will the system be able to process the necessary quantity of data with the desired speed and accuracy?

Implications for Management

The single most important implication of the dynamic life cycle of a project is that which relates to the way in which the project should be managed. It would be very difficult for a line manager in marketing or data processing to manage an

MMIS development project within the confines of his operating organization, with its existing relationships and its existing patterns of authority and responsibility. This is so because virtually no operating bureaucracy is equipped to deal with the constant change inherent in the project life cycle. Operating organizations—marketing, sales, advertising, etc.—are established to perform specific functions on a continuing basis. While their methods, procedures, workloads, and other elements do indeed change over time, the change is usually gradual; if not, it requires reorganization of the function to cope with a radically different set of problems or procedures.

The MMIS development project will, by its very nature, involve significant and radical changes in resources, skills, activities, procedures, etc., throughout the life cycle. To try to manage such a dynamic activity through an operations-oriented functional organization would throw that organization into chaos, and it would not be likely to achieve either its operational or functional objectives or its MMIS project objectives.

Of course, one might argue that the project should be performed within the function of data processing or of the information system. After all, they do this all of the time, don't they?

The answer is only a qualified yes. One must remember that even those in the information system "business" have the same variety of operating responsibilities as do marketing people. They are in the business of *operating* information systems, updating files, revising programs, etc.—all the things that are essential to keeping the organization's current information systems chugging along and producing useful output. Thus, the same problem exists in the information system function as in the marketing function.

The answer to this organizational dilemma would then appear to be the giving of responsibility for the MMIS design and development to some group outside the functional organizations of the marketing or information systems. Such a group would presumably be able to avoid the divided loyalties which exist for a functional manager who is trying to balance his operating responsibilities with his project-developing ones. Moreover, such a group could be as dynamic in its size and composition as the project requires.

These are the basic ideas underlying the concept of a *project team* which is headed by a *project manager*.

Project Management

The idea of project management emanated from the World War II days of the Manhattan Project atomic bomb development project. The idea has been greatly advanced and widely applied in a variety of industries and areas, including the U.S. moon exploration project and the development projects for all major military weapons systems and most major innovations in management systems such as the MMIS.

The basic concept of project management is, perhaps, best exemplified by Figure 9-1 in which a traditional functional marketing department and a data processing department comprise the vertical organization. These are the operating departments which do the day-to-day business of their particular function. The vertical arrows below each data processing and marketing function suggest that authority and responsibility patterns in these organizations run up and down the chain of command. Salespeople are responsible only to the sales manager, who is, in turn, solely responsible to the marketing manager. A keypunch operator is responsible to the section supervisor, who is, in turn, responsible to the data preparation manager, etc.

The MMIS project manager is shown outside this vertical organization with a set of authority and responsibility patterns which run horizontally across all the various functions of data processing and marketing (and perhaps some others as well). The job of the project manager is to pull together the resources which are necessary to get the MMIS development job done. The job has no operating responsibilities, although in some small organizations the project manager may wear two hats and operate in this capacity only on a part-time basis. However, for the role of project manager, *the objective is simple and clearcut—to get the system developed in a fashion which meets cost, time, and performance objectives.*

To do this, the project manager draws on the resources of the marketing and data processing organizations. During some phases of the project life cycle, the project manager may request the full-time assignment of various marketing and data processing people to the MMIS project team. During other phases, these people may serve on a part-time basis, a consultative basis, or not at all, depending on the need for their skills and the input information which they can provide.

The job of project managers is a difficult one, since they operate within the framework of the vertical functional organizations which, after all, have always existed and will continue to exist long after the MMIS development project is gone and forgotten. Moreover, they have no direct authority over the functional manager who must provide them with the personnel necessary for accomplishing their mission.

However, they also operate within the framework of an overall organizational commitment to the MMIS development effort. Thus, *they are responsible for a major organizational effort to which all operating managers must have previously committed their support.* The project manager, therefore, has great powers of moral suasion, if not legal authority, and must know how to use these powers to obtain the resources that are needed at the time they are needed.

The circled intersections of vertical and horizontal lines in Figure 9-1 represent the interfaces between functional and project managers, and between func-

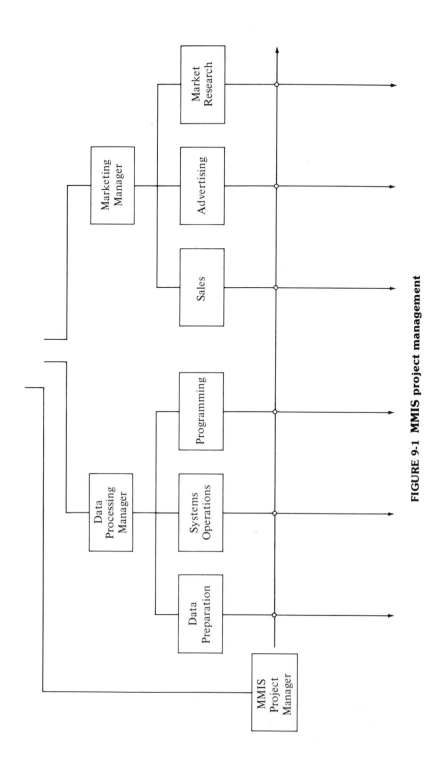

FIGURE 9-1 MMIS project management

TABLE 9-6 The Project and Function Interface *

Project Manager	Functional Manager
What is to be done?	How will the task be done?
When will the task be done?	Where will the task be done?
Why will the task be done?	Who will do the task?
How much money is available to do the task?	How well has the functional input been integrated into the project?
How well has the total project been done?	

* From David I. Cleland and William R. King, *Systems Analysis and Project Management,* 2d ed. (New York: McGraw-Hill, 1975), p. 237. Used with permission.

tional and project *goals* as well. The project manager must operate through those interfaces to achieve project goals.

In another context, the author and his colleague provided the definition of the project and function interface shown in Table 9-6. The table suggests appropriate rules for project and functional managers working together to achieve project goals.

The table shows that the project manager is responsible for things which concern the overall achievement of project goals and the integration of functional activities to achieve those goals. The functional manager is responsible for the area of expertise in a particular function, as it relates to the project, and for the assignment of personnel to it.

For instance, the functional manager in marketing decides who will be assigned to work with analysts to delineate information needs and also how and where project tasks are to be done. Definition of the tasks to be performed in a particular marketing function are necessary, for example, in developing the descriptive LRC model of Chapter 7. The project manager will decide *what* is to be done (e.g., whether to use the LRC model approach); but the marketing manager will decide on the substance of the marketing inputs to the model. This is done through the marketing representative for the project.

Planning the Project

The manager of the MMIS development project should begin by establishing a project plan consisting of a *project proposal, work breakdown structure, network plan, project schedule,* and *project budget.* [1]

[1] Ibid. Appendix 1 gives a detailed outline of a comprehensive project plan which incorporates these elements as well as many others.

Project proposal

The project proposal is a basic document used to generate the interest of management in, and, hopefully, the support of management for, the MMIS. Usually, this will be the first document prepared in the conceptual stage of the project's life cycle.

In some organizations, a project proposal is prepared, and after it is approved, detailed schedules, budgets, and the other plan elements are developed under the framework provided in the proposal. This is the "top down" approach which provides ample opportunity for the preparation of alternative proposals among which management is to choose. In other organizations, especially those in which general approval of the MMIS has already been given and its general nature is already known, the detailed planning documents are prepared to support the proposal. This way provides greater realism, but less opportunity for change since most people see such a detailed plan as already being cast in concrete with little opportunity for consideration of alternatives.

In either case, the project proposal should contain the following items:

1. Statement of the need for the system
2. Objectives of the MMIS
3. System description, cost, and performance expectations
4. Statement of the assumptions underlying the items in number 3, in terms of who will use the system, who will support its development, etc.
5. Summary plan of the project in terms of budget, personnel, schedule, etc.
6. Summaries of benefits to be expected from the system and costs to be incurred
7. Specification of required management actions

Such a proposal will usually be in written form with an appropriate executive summary at the beginning and supporting data, charts, graphs, etc., in appendices. Usually, briefing sessions will be conducted with top management to obtain their support, so the specifications of management actions may have to be changed depending on whether top management is being asked for financial support or functional managers are being asked for their commitment to support the project in the fashion described in Figure 9-1 and Table 9-6.

Work breakdown structure

The work breakdown structure is a basic planning device which requires the manager to *decompose* the system development project into its constituent elements and subelements. This allows for the precise definition of tasks which must be performed and the subsequent planning for who will do them, how long they can be expected to take, and what relationship each task will have with every other one.

Usually a work breakdown structure is constructed in chart form by relating each major subsystem to its constituent subsystems, each subsystem to tasks which must be performed, and each task to a work package. A work package is a specific job which contributes to a specific task on the path to the accomplishment of the overall system objective. A work package may involve the completion of a design, the providing of a document, the specification of a set of information requirements, on the performance of a service.

Project network plans

Once a work breakdown structure has been developed, project network plans can be prepared. Network plans represent projects in terms of the interrelationships among the critical project elements. These pictorial displays are constructed around the technological and time requirements of a project in a way which separates the planning and scheduling functions. This permits the consideration of alternative plans. When scheduling is subsequently performed, it may be done on the basis of the availability of resources and the demands of other projects.

With more traditional techniques, a linear calendar format is used. This forces the schedule to be prepared simultaneously with the project plan. The technological and time-requirement aspects of project planning become intermingled with the resource-allocation problems of scheduling. As a result, alternative plans are usually evaluated on the basis of their schedules. Furthermore, because planning and scheduling proceed in a step-by-step fashion, trade-offs between planning and scheduling cannot be determined so as to arrive at a preferred course of action.

Only a small percentage of the tasks and jobs are critical to the overall time requirement for completing most projects. Furthermore, tasks which are critical in one plan may not be critical in another, and noncritical tasks may become critical because of the way they are scheduled. Knowing which tasks are critical to a project plan facilitates scheduling the project and allocating the resources necessary to accomplish it. Scheduling the critical jobs first will usually permit considerable latitude in scheduling the remainder.

The simplest network plan is a *precedence diagram,* which simply depicts major project elements in terms of their sequential relationships; for example, which must be finished before others may start and which cannot be started until others are finished. The most widely known and used network plan is the critical path network which is the basis for PERT, or Program Evaluation and Review Technique. We shall not go into the details of PERT here because it is more widely discussed in textbooks than used in actual practice.

The author has seen many MMIS project network plans which are large enough to cover all of the walls of a large room and which are so detailed as to require rather close scrutiny even by someone with 20-20 vision. The highly simplified example of such a network plan shown in Figure 9-2 is a toy by comparison, and is provided for illustrative purposes only.

Figure 9-2 shows some of the major tasks which might be involved in the early stages of an MMIS project. The numbers in parentheses represent the best estimate, in weeks, of how long each activity will take. It shows that a first step (activity 1-2) is a study of company objectives and strategies. This activity is carried on concurrently with an identification of marketing problems (activity 1-3). Both activities must be completed, as shown by the dotted arrows, before activity 4-5, developing a gross design concept, can be begun. Once this is done, the two parallel activities to specify information needs and to specify subsystems (activity 5-6 and activity 5-7) can begin. These two activities plus activity 6-8, the testing and evaluating of needs (which can take place only after the needs have been identified), must all be completed before the preparation of the proposal can begin.

One can readily see how a network plan requires a detailed specification of the various project tasks and their relationship and how, as well, it permits other project planning such as scheduling and budgeting.[2]

Project schedules

Project schedules may be readily developed from the network plan using time estimates for each of the activities represented on the plan. For instance, if activities 1-2 and 1-3 in Figure 9-2 are expected to require 2 and 3 weeks respectively, event 4 cannot occur for at least 3 weeks, since it cannot occur until *both* these activities have been completed. Thus, the development of the gross design concept (activity 4-5) cannot be scheduled to *begin* until 3 weeks have elapsed.

A quick glance through the network shows that event 5 cannot take place earlier than 5 weeks nor event 8 earlier than 8 weeks from the beginning of the project. This is so because the *critical path*—the longest path through the network—is of 8 weeks duration. (The critical path can be seen to be the one going through event numbers 1, 3, 4, 5, 6, and 8.)

The critical path through the network determines the minimum project duration as well as the earliest time that any event may be scheduled. Hence, the network and the analyses of the time estimates provide the basis for project scheduling.

[2] Ibid., chap. 15, for a detailed treatment of network plans and other project planning techniques.

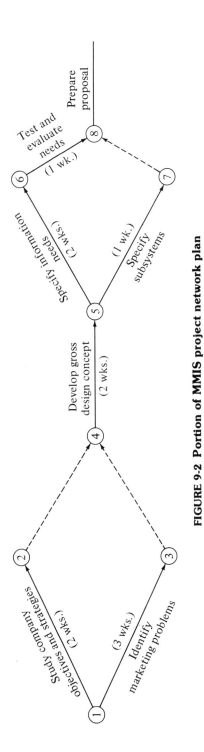

FIGURE 9-2 Portion of MMIS project network plan

Project budget

Determination of the project schedule and budget requires that those who will perform each task be identified and that the duration of each activity be estimated. Thus, the personnel budget follows directly from the network plan, since it merely involves accounting calculations based on salary rates, fringe benefit rates, etc.

The other elements of the budget (equipment, supplies, etc.) are readily developed. However, only *direct costs* are usually incorporated into project budgets, since these are the only costs over which the project manager has control.

Controlling the Project

Once the project has been thoroughly planned and gets underway, the emphasis of the project manager's job shifts from planning to control, ensuring that the project meets its time, cost, and performance objectives.

To permit managers to exercise such control, it is necessary that they develop a *project management information system* (PMIS). That is, they need an information system to control a project which itself involves the development of a marketing management information system! Of course, the PMIS is undoubtedly going to be much less complex and sophisticated than the MMIS, otherwise it will itself require that a major development project be undertaken.

The basic purpose of the PMIS is the facilitation of control. This is achieved through the timely reporting of cost, time, and performance levels for the various work packages, tasks and subsystems. If one of these is out of control (over cost, behind schedule, or severely deviating from planned performance levels), the project manager must take action to get the system back into control.

This may be done in any of a variety of ways, for example, by providing more resources, replacing responsible personnel, revising schedules, or revising performance standards. The crucial point is that the manager must be able to identify and recognize project areas that are out of control and to take action to rectify the situations *before they become major problems which endanger the overall success of the project.*

Because the overall success of the project is the project manager's primary concern, the critical activities (those on the critical path in the network plan) are of primary concern. This is so because delays in critical activities will cause delays in the overall project, because of the very nature of the activities, whereas delays in noncritical activities will not necessarily delay the overall project. Thus, project managers have, in the form of the network plan, an effective device for management by exception. They can focus their primary attention on managing the critical activities and devote less attention to the noncritical ones because they know that these can "hurt less" in the pursuit of overall project goals.

This means that the project manager must "replan" the project when critical activities get out of control. Often, this takes the form of reallocating people or funds from noncritical activities to out-of-control critical ones. The project manager hopes that by so doing he will not lengthen the critical path and thus delay the overall project. He also knows that by doing so he will probably lengthen the time required on those noncritical activities which he has "robbed" of resources. In doing so, he may have created a monster by making another path critical. Thus, he must carefully replan the project using the network plan to balance the various paths in a way that ensures the best possible schedule performance.

Summary

Every complex system, such as an MMIS, goes through a system life cycle. This life cycle reflects the constantly changing activities, resource demands, and levels of activity inherent in the design, development and installation of an MMIS.

The dynamic nature of the life cycle of the system's development usually dictates that the development project be pursued in some way that goes beyond the typical functional structure of the organization. This is so because relevant functional organizations such as the marketing and data processing departments must devote their major attention to their operating responsibilities rather than to an MMIS development effort, which may have future benefit but do nothing immediate to make their job easier. Without some project organization for the MMIS, the MMIS effort will necessarily be given low priority by functional organizations, however great may be its potential value.

The concept of project management as applied to MMIS development establishes a single individual, the project manager, as the one responsible for managing the critical *cost, time,* and *performance* parameters of the MMIS development effort. Functional managers, such as the marketing manager and the data processing manager, are placed in clear-cut supportive roles relative to this effort. Their responsibilities are for the *substance* of their functional input (the *how, where, who,* and *how well* aspects), whereas the project manager is concerned with the *administrative* aspects (the *what, when, why* and *how much* aspects).

In planning the MMIS development project, the project manager must develop a project proposal, which is used to generate interest in the system concept, and various administrative planning tools such as a work breakdown structure, a network plan, a project schedule, and a project budget. As the project ensues, project control is also facilitated by these devices, since they permit the assessment of progress and the reallocation of resources to meet changing circumstances.

EXERCISES

1. Other life cycle concepts are closely related to the life cycle of the system's development. For instance, the product sales life cycle describes the life of a product in terms of its sales performance. Construct a graphical description of such a life cycle and describe its various phases.

2. How do the implications which one might draw from the product sales life cycle relate to those which may be drawn from the system development life cycle? Relate this to the job of the product manager.

3. Relate the conceptual phase of the system development life cycle to the preparation of the MMIS project proposal.

4. Which phases of the system development life cycle relate, generally, to the general and detailed design phases for an MMIS?

5. Describe the production or acquisition phase and the operational phase of the system development life cycle in information system terminology.

6. Relate the evolutionary design principle to the divestment phase of the system development life cycle in terms of the specifics of Table 9-5.

7. Describe the need for the project team and project management design and development approach in achieving an effective MMIS.

8. Tell what the following statement means: Project measures of cost, time, and performance involve trade-offs by the project manager.

9. What is the project manager's authority with respect to the functional manager?

10. What is the ultimate basis for resolving conflict between the project manager and the functional manager? (See Figure 9-1.)

11. If the method of resolving conflict in question 10 were frequently used, what do you think would happen?

12. Relate the project proposal to the documents described in Chapter 8 as the outputs of the detailed design phase of the system.

13. A Gantt chart is a bar chart in which various project activities are listed along the left side and time periods are marked off across a sheet of paper. The bars then represent a schedule for each activity. Construct such a chart and compare it with the network plan of Figure 9-2. What are the advantages and limitations of each?

14. Make a change in one activity time estimate in Figure 9-2 in such a way as to change the critical path.

15. Develop a project schedule for your project plan, as revised in question 14.

16. Suppose that a critical activity in Figure 9-2 is going to run one week over the estimate given there. What might the project manager do?

REFERENCES

Anshen, M., "The Management of Ideas." *Harvard Business Review,* July–August 1969.

Carlson, W. M. "A Management Information System Designed by Managers." *Datamation,* May 1967, pp. 37–43.

Cleland, David I. "Organizational Concepts of Project Management." *IEEE Transactions on Engineering Management,* December 1966.

——— and King, William R. *Systems Analysis and Project Management,* 2d ed. New York: McGraw-Hill, 1975.

Drucker, P. F. "New Templates for Today's Organizations." *Harvard Business Review,* January–February 1974.

Evans, M. K., and Hague, L. R. "Master Plan for Information Systems." *Harvard Business Review,* January–February 1962.

Goggin, W. C. "How the Multidimensional Structure Works at Dow Corning." *Harvard Business Review,* January–February 1974.

Hax, A. C. "Planning a Management Information System for a Distributing and Manufacturing Company." *Sloan Management Review,* Spring 1973, pp. 85–98.

McFarlan, F. W. "Problems in Planning the Information System." *Harvard Business Review,* March–April 1971, pp. 74–89.

Powers, R. F. and Dickson, G. W. "MIS Project Management: Myths, Opinions and Reality." *Californial Management Review,* Spring 1973, pp. 147–156.

Schwartz, M. K. "MIS Planning." *Datamation,* September 1970, pp. 28–31.

10

The Future of MMIS [1]

[1] Portions of this chapter are adapted from the author's paper. "The Intelligent MIS—A Management Helper," *Business Horizons*, October 1973, with permission of the publisher.

The variety of MMIS which has been discussed in previous chapters is a rather sophisticated decision-oriented one which is beyond the state of the art that exists in many firms today. However, even this variety of MMIS is a lineal descendant of manual information systems and the computerized information systems of the past few decades. In this chapter, we seek to sum up the characteristics which distinguish the sophisticated MMIS from data processing systems and other less sophisticated systems. In addition, we shall address the future of the MMIS and the future of the entire range of information systems in terms of new system concepts which will provide radically new capabilities for systems in supporting a broad range of managerial activities.[2]

In making these projections for the future, we shall resist the temptation to employ the wild creativity of a science fiction writer, and we shall limit our discussion of future systems to those already under development or those for which the seeds of research have already been planted.

A State-of-the-Art MMIS

The MMIS that has been discussed in previous chapters is not typical of the state of the art in most real-world organizations. A few organizations have developed such a system in total, some organizations have developed it in part, and most organizations have only begun to develop it. Its description, therefore, is given in terms of technical and managerial feasibility rather than in terms of real-world practice.

However much the MMIS concepts of this book may appear to be futuristic to those who cannot conceive of computer systems which do more than replace manual clerical operations, students of MMIS should not be misled into believing that this variety of MMIS is too "far out." Today's students will live in the future, and they will be increasingly challenged to develop and to utilize systems such as those described here. Indeed, in the not-too-distant future, they will be challenged beyond anything that has thus far been described, as we shall note later in this chapter.

The critical MMIS characteristics and issues which should be on the minds of such MMIS students, be they students enrolled in courses or managers who have not yet discovered all of the answers, can be summed up rather concisely in the following set of questions. The form presented constitutes a checklist for assessing the degree to which an information system, either existing or contemplated, reflects characteristics of an up-to-date *management* information system.

---

[2] Because of this, we shall use the acronym MIS in this chapter.

1. Are we using information to support decisions, or are we merely processing it?
2. Is our system designed from the viewpoint of decision support, or is such support viewed as a by-product?
3. Does our MMIS support strategic decisions as well as operational and management control decisions?
4. Has information which is to be incorporated into the system been assessed on a cost/value basis?
5. Have the information requirements of managers been assessed in terms of the specific decisions from which those requirements emanate?
6. Have alternative structures for the system been assessed, and have various useful concepts of the structure of the system been simultaneously incorporated into the MMIS?
7. Have opportunities been considered for a wide range of subsystems which can enable the organization to cope better with an ever-changing environment?
8. Has the system been designed from the viewpoint of its manager-users rather than from that of information systems technicians?
9. Does the system provide managers with the minimum information which is necessary for them to be effective?
10. Is the overall system cost-effective?
11. Is the system design evolutionary, so that system changes will be facilitated rather than hindered?
12. Are the system objectives directly related to the overall objectives of the organization?
13. Has the system been designed in parallel with redesigned organizational practices and procedures rather than simply to serve an existing, and possibly outmoded, organization?
14. Has the effort to develop the system design proceeded according to a plan which related each system element to every other one and which required that each element be justified for incorporation into the system?
15. Has an organization been developed which can successfully design and develop the system in the context of the operating realities of the overall organization?
16. Is the system's design-development project being managed in the same careful way that other organizational activities are managed?

An MMIS which can meet the test of these questions is one which reflects the best of current knowledge about management information systems. One that cannot meet these tests probably is an already obsolete system, which will become apparent only too rapidly as the future unfolds.

The Intelligent System

The idea of information systems which serve their human master carried over directly from the design concepts of data processing to those of management information systems which provide more sophisticated information backup to managers. Thus, even though an MIS may be much more extensive in scope and more intimately related to decision making than the data system which preceded it, its role as a servant of the manager may be identical.

Several contemporary developments would appear to foretell of a new and expanded role for the MIS. This new role is one in which the system takes on the role of an intelligent helper, rather than of a servant. In such a capacity, the MIS would truly complement the manager in that it would not simply respond to his requests, but, rather, would aid him in structuring problems and understanding the environment in which he operates.

Of course, such predictions have previously been made by numerous respected authorities.[3] Many of those ambitious assessments made in the early 1960s concerning the role which computers would play in the 1970s have not come to pass. However, with the advent of fourth-generation computer systems, it would appear that hardware technology has outstripped software technology and that further developments of more sophisticated MIS are now up to MIS specialists rather than to computer hardware developers.

This is a rather new state of affairs in the evolution of the computer era, and it augers favorably for the development of a more sophisticated MIS. Taken together with new developments in the field of artificial intelligence, this new state of affairs would appear to indicate that the intelligent MIS is on the horizon.

Basic MIS information model

The basic MIS model which governs the intelligent MIS is shown in Figure 10-1. It involves rather straightforward basic communication links between the manager, the MIS, and the operating environment. The unique aspect of the model is the *nature* of the information flowing along these linkages.

For instance, the manager-to-computer link has the manager providing the computer with subjective probabilities, evaluated performance data, and system axioms. The computer-to-manager link shows the manager being provided with such information items as proposed models, revised probabilities, and evaluated strategies. Almost all the information flows shown in Figure 10-1 are varieties which are foreign to state-of-the-art information systems. They represent the essence of the new variety of intelligent MIS.

---

[3] See, for example, John Diebold, *Beyond Automation* (New York: McGraw-Hill, 1964) and H. J. Leavitt and T. L. Whisler, "Management in the 1980s," *Harvard Business Review,* November–December 1958, pp. 41–48.

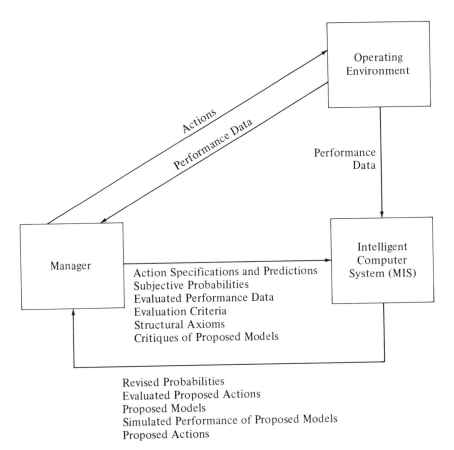

Actions

Performance Data

Operating
Environment

Performance
Data

Manager

Intelligent
Computer
System (MIS)

Action Specifications and Predictions
Subjective Probabilities
Evaluated Performance Data
Evaluation Criteria
Structural Axioms
Critiques of Proposed Models

Revised Probabilities
Evaluated Proposed Actions
Proposed Models
Simulated Performance of Proposed Models
Proposed Actions

FIGURE 10-1 Basic model for the intelligent MIS

These unusual information flows are best explained in terms of several technologies which have developed in recent years to the point that they may now be considered feasible for inclusion into the operating MIS. In discussing each of these technologies, reference will be made to the specific elements of information in Figure 10-1. However, before proceeding to a discussion of these technologies, we must distinguish among the various varieties of intelligent MIS.

An MIS taxonomy

The various intelligence-related technologies are directly related to important levels of sophistication of management information systems of both the "standard" and intelligent variety.

Figure 10-2 shows the MIS taxonomy, previously given in Chapter 3, which

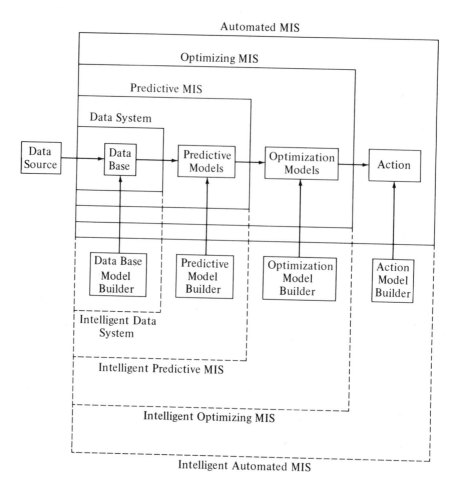

FIGURE 10-2 MIS taxonomy

is based on the role played by models in the MIS. The basic horizontal flow in the figure shows a decision process represented in terms of various stages.[4] Thus, in any decision situation, data from a source are collected and aggregated into a data base. Then, predictive models, such as sales forecasting models, may be applied to these data. At a more advanced level, optimization models, which determine the best course of action in a particular situation, may be utilized. Lastly, action must be taken.

Any or all of these steps in decision making may be included as an element

[4] The horizontal flow in Figure 10-2 is adapted from William R. King and David I. Cleland, "Manager-Analyst Teamwork in MIS Design," *Business Horizons,* April 1971. Their version is, in turn, adapted from R. O. Mason, Jr., "Basic Concepts for Designing Management Information Systems," AIS Research Paper No. 8, Graduate School of Administration, UCLA, October 1969.

of an MIS. Those stages not formally incorporated into any particular MIS represent functions which are left for the manager to perform. These various man-machine interfaces are described and evaluated in Chapter 3.

These ideas can be expanded to define a hierarchy of information systems. The taxonomy is hierarchical in that each successive system incorporates all elements of the previous systems as well as the specific technology which serves to define it. The hierarchy is as follows:

Data system

Predictive MIS

Optimizing MIS

Automated MIS

Intelligent data system

Intelligent predictive MIS

Intelligent optimizing MIS

Intelligent automated MIS

As shown in Figure 10-2 by the solid block labeled *data system,* such a system is one which incorporates only the data base element of the decision process. Thus, it takes data from some source and aggregates, categorizes, and synthesizes them for presentation to the decision maker. All of the other steps in the decision process are performed manually by the manager. Such a system is truly the servant of the manager, since it usually provides him only with fixed reports of historical events at specified reporting intervals.

The figure shows that a *predictive MIS* incorporates predictive models as well as a data base into the physical system. For instance, an MIS which includes sales forecasting models, so that the manager is provided with projections of the future as well as with records of the past, is such a system.

An *optimizing MIS* includes optimization models which prescribe the best action for the manager to take as well as incorporating all the capabilities of the lower systems. The operational systems for scheduling oil refineries based on complex computerized linear programming models are illustrative of this variety of MIS.

The *automated MIS* is that in which all the steps from data base to action are performed within the system, that is, the action to be taken is *determined and executed* within the system rather than by the manager. Of course, such systems are in operation only for simple decisions. For instance, inventory control systems which monitor stock levels, determine optimal reorder quantities, and type out a purchase order for mailing can be considered to be of this variety.

The *intelligent MIS* incorporates an additional dimension—that of a model builder. The key to this idea is that all the previous systems, whatever the degree of sophistication of the models which they entail, presume that the models are constructed by human beings outside the system. Usually this role is reserved for operations research analysts or forecasting experts.

Model building within the MIS. The various types of intelligent MIS incorporate a model building capability within the system. The four different varieties of the intelligent MIS are distinguished by the nature of their model building capacity—data base model building, predictive model building, optimization model building, or action model building. These various intelligent systems are shown in Figure 10-2 by dotted-line extensions of the basic systems. Thus, the creation of an *intelligent data system* involves the addition of a data base model builder to a data system. Similarly, an *intelligent predictive MIS* incorporates four elements—data base, predictive models, data base model builder and predictive model builder; while a predictive MIS incorporates only the first two of these elements.

Of course, in distinguishing among these eight varieties of information systems, one must recognize that different degrees of sophistication are feasible for different decision problems. Thus, while the intelligent automated MIS is currently operational for some low-level problems, even data base systems have not yet been developed for some high-level strategic decisions.

The hierarchy of information systems developed here does not, therefore, assume that all problems are subject to the same level of treatment using an MIS. An intelligent MIS may be built which is intelligent only for one kind of problem while treating other problems at less sophisticated levels. Thus, all mixtures are feasible, and those systems which will be developed in the next few years will almost certainly be of the hybrid variety.

To further define the elements of this taxonomy, we now turn to the various technologies related to each: the data organizational, learning, automated problem-solving and abductive technologies.

Data organizational technology

One aspect of intelligence which needs to be considered briefly is that related to the organization of data. The data base model builder in Figure 10-2 is meant to imply that the system involves a capability for structuring and managing the storage of data in the data base.

Data base management systems which perform this function to various degrees are already well developed and commercially available. Such systems provide a resolution to some of the difficulties created by the different requirements for the same data which are typically generated by various system users and also file structures which will accommodate these different requirements, file processing software, access methods, etc.

Although there is a great need for further development of such models, the basic computer technology is well known and already applied. We, therefore, choose to emphasize here the other less-developed technologies as they are related to more sophisticated aspects of system intelligence.[5]

Learning technology

One of the basic qualities which a truly intelligent system must possess is a *learning capability*. To learn from experience requires two key elements: an ability to revise models automatically based on actual experience, and a feedforward loop from the manager to the system. This learning capability is directly related to the development of predictive model-builders for use in an *intelligent predictive MIS*.

The basic technology for the first element has already been developed in several contexts and with several different foci. For instance, the forecasting technique called exponentially weighted moving averages [6] uses a model which takes account of the *difference* between the forecast made for the most recent time period and the actual value observed in that period in determining the forecast for the next time period. This predictive technology thus recognizes the need to learn by constantly updating the predictive model being used, and to explicitly take account of the forecasting errors of the past in making new predictions.[7]

Another technology which can be thought of in this sense is that of Bayesian analysis. The key element of Bayesian predictive models is the provision of a capability for the revision of likelihood assessments made by the manager as actual experience develops. Although there is no intrinsic link between the two concepts, Bayesian analysis is often applied to the subjective probabilities assessments made by managers concerning the likelihood of future events. Thus, Figure 10-1 shows subjective probabilities being provided to the MIS by the manager. These probabilities are his subjective estimates of the likelihood related to specified future events such as a workers' strike or "sales over $2 million." Based on data obtained directly from the operating environment, these prior probabilities are revised by the MIS into posterior probabilities based on both the manager's prior judgment and the data from real-world events. The Bayesian model is the basis for making these revisions.[8]

---

[5] For further discussion of data management systems, see J. F. Kelly, *Computerized Management Information Systems* (New York: Macmillan, 1970), chap. 8.

[6] See R. G. Brown and R. F. Meyer, "The Fundamental Theorem of Exponential Smoothing," *Operations Research,* September–October 1961, pp. 673–680.

[7] A similar approach in a predictive problem involving network planning is taken in William R. King and T. A. Wilson, "Subjective Time Estimates in Critical Path Planning—A Preliminary Analysis," *Management Science,* vol. 13, no. 5 (January 1967).

[8] For a discussion of Bayesian analysis as applied to management decision problems, see William R. King, *Probability for Management Decisions* (New York: Wiley, 1968), chap. 12.

Feedforward loops. However, before technologies such as these can truly be thought of as capable of learning, they must be complemented with a feedforward loop from the manager to the MIS. The feedforward aspect of learning simply means that the system must be provided with both real-world data on events which have occurred *and the manager's evaluation of them*. The contemporary MIS incorporates *feedback* to the manager on how his actions have affected the environment. It usually does not include the feedforward element of information provided *to the system* concerning the manager's evaluation, or interpretation of this feedback. For instance, suppose the manager takes an action based on a prediction of the demand for his product, only to find that sales do not meet expectations. The system must be provided with a specification of the action taken, the prediction on which it was based, as well as performance data from the real world—the first two elements being provided by the manager and the latter by the environment as shown in Figure 10-1.

In order that the system possess a real learning capability, it must even be provided with additional information. Was the failure to meet expectations the fault of the prediction or due to special circumstances (e.g., a strike)? What is the manager's interpretation of the variance? (Is it within an acceptable limit?) Does the manager consider the performance level to be good or bad?

The technology for providing this feedforward linkage to the MIS is not complex; however, it has not been widely operationalized. For instance, as shown in Figure 10-1, it requires that qualitative evaluations of objective performance data and evaluation criteria be incorporated into the data base.

Models such as those of multiple discriminant analysis can also be incorporated into the MIS to utilize these qualitative evaluations in objectively analyzing the appropriateness of various performance criteria.[9]

Automatic problem-solving technology

Another aspect of intelligence is required for the development of even more sophisticated varieties of the intelligent MIS. This element, referred to here as the problem-solving technology, is best illustrated by *automatic theorem proving*.

Automatic theorem-proving techniques have been developed in the context of the proof of mathematical theorems—statements of valid relationships among mathematical quantities. However, they are applicable to a wide variety of situations which relate to management decisions.

The basis for the proof of a mathematical theorem is a set of *axioms*, or relevant statements which are known to be true. A *conjecture* is posed by the mathematician and then tested for validity by logical comparison with the set of ax-

[9] This approach is described in William R. King, "Performance Evaluation in Marketing Systems," *Management Science*, July 1964.

ioms. If the conjecture can be shown to be valid, it is a theorem—a valid statement of a relationship which can be added to the store of mathematical knowledge.

The analogy of management decisions is straightforward. Suppose that the axiom set expresses relationships among machine capacities, product machining requirements, resource availabilities and previously scheduled tasks. A conjecture concerning the scheduling of a new task on this equipment can be logically tested for validity against this set of relationships. If it is shown to be valid, the proposed schedule is known to be feasible. If not, another schedule can be conjectured and tested.

A wide variety of other problems can be dealt with in this fashion. For instance, the question of assessing the congruence of a proposed objective, as stated by or for an organizational element, with the overall set of interrelated organizational policies, goals, objectives and environmental constraints, is also a theorem-proving exercise.

The main thing about automatic theorem proving as it relates to the intelligent MIS is that a purely mechanical procedure has been developed, using a technique called resolution, so that the system can perform the proof.[10]

This approach represents the most basic operational approach both to the development of optimization model builders and to the advanced development of predictive model builders. To operationalize this technology in this fashion within an intelligent MIS requires, as shown in Figure 10-1, that the system be provided with basic structural relationships and system axioms by the manager. These relationships include such things as machine capacities, previously scheduled jobs, and job machining requirements in the production scheduling example; and basic statements of objectives, policies, and goals in the goal congruence example. In turn, the system can evaluate proposed actions and provide such evaluations to the manager.

Abductive technology

The element of intelligence which is most crucial to the development of intelligent management information systems relates to the basic process of developing the structure of the decision system. If the manager is fully aware of all the relationships governing the operation of any system, he is probably reasonably able to understand and manage the system without the aid of sophisticated varieties of MIS. It is only when the system becomes too complex (as with those situations where automatic theorem proving is useful) or where the manager lacks a full understanding of the intricacies of its operation that such systems become essential.

[10] See J. J. Nilsson, *Problem-Solving Methods in Artificial Intelligence* (New York: McGraw-Hill, 1971), chap. 6.

In such situations, the manager needs to be able to put it all together conceptually, to develop his own understanding of the system to a degree where he is able to give adequate consideration to the various interactions and interrelationships which exist. To complement the manager in developing this sort of model, the MIS must have some abductive capability.

Abduction, sometimes called hypothesis, is a mode of reasoning which differs from the more formalized modes of deduction and induction. Essentially this mode of reasoning begins with symptoms and develops hypotheses which *could* explain these symptoms. According to Peirce:

> Hypothesis is where we find some very curious circumstance, which would be explained by the supposition that it was a case of a certain general rule, and thereupon adopt that supposition. Or, where we find that in certain respects two objects have a strong resemblance, and infer that they resemble one another strongly in other respects.[11]

This method of reasoning is essentially one of constructing explanations for observed phenonema based on a partial understanding of the system being dealt with. Pople and Werner [12] have developed computer software and applied abductive reasoning concepts in medical diagnosis using the basic logical principles of theorem proving. Extensions to other areas of problem solving, where the medical language of symptoms and diagnosis are not commonly used, but indeed apply, are being developed.

In operationalizing this variety of intelligence in an MIS, the basic technology of theorem proving is directly useful. The axioms of the system represent statements of the partial understanding of system relationships which are held by managers. The conjecture becomes a set of observations of system performance in this frame of reference. The objective of the automatic theorem prover is to generate an explanation of the observed phenomena. This explanation, or proposed model, can then be evaluated by the manager. His evaluation leads to critiques, as shown in Figure 10-1. These critiques may represent either new relationships to add to the axiomatic base or, in more advanced applications, input for the criteria which are used by the theorem prover in selecting among alternative feasible models for presentation to the manager.

The creative aspect of intelligence

The most advanced step in the development of an *automated intelligent MIS* is the development of a creative aspect of intelligence within the system. This is in-

---

[11] See C. S. Peirce, "Ampliative Reasoning," *Collected Papers of C. S. Peirce*, vol. II, chap. 5, Cambridge, Mass.: Harvard University Press (Belknap Press).

[12] H. Pople and G. Werner, *An Information Processing Approach to Theory Formation in Biomedical Research*, "AFIPS Conference Proceedings," Spring Joint Computer Conference, vol. 40 (May 1972).

terpreted here in the context of an action model builder, an automated device for the generation of alternative actions to be considered by the decision maker.

In all the myriad approaches to decision analysis, the specification of the alternatives to be considered is left to the manager. The best developed organized approaches to creativity are such subjective processes as brainstorming. Other processes which have been computerized simply involve the generation of alternatives which are permutations and combinations of other alternatives, rather than the generation of truly creative ones.[13]

The best current hope for such systems would appear to be imbedded in those technologies previously discussed. For instance, the creation of new action alternatives is implicit in the creation of new models of the system. Hence the abductive approach would appear to be adaptable to this requirement.

In any case, the creative aspect of intelligence, which is the last step in developing the most sophisticated MIS, is not well developed. Perhaps it is never to be.

However, from the point of view of the existing operational MIS, the various levels of the intelligent MIS which do appear to be feasible—*intelligent data system, intelligent predictive MIS*, and *intelligent optimizing MIS*—are much beyond the boundaries of current practice. The optimist can only hope that as such systems are developed, a better understanding of the creative process will be developed. If that is the case, "HAL," the intelligent automated MIS of the movie *2001: A Space Odyssey*, may be at hand.

REFERENCES

Brown, R. G., and Meyer, R. F. "The Fundamental Theorem of Exponential Smoothing." *Operations Research*, September–October 1961, pp. 673–680.

Cardenas, A.; Presser, L.; and Marin, M. *Computer Science*. New York: Wiley, 1972.

Cooper, D. C. "Theorem Proving in Computers." In L. Fox, ed., *Advances in Programming and Non-Numerical Computation*. New York: Pergamon Press, 1966.

Guard, J. R., et al. "Semi-Automated Mathematics." *Journal of the Association for Computing Machinery* 16 (January 1969): 49–62.

Kelly, J. F. *Computerized Management Information Systems*. New York: Macmillan, 1970, chap. 8.

King, William R. *Probability for Management Decisions*. New York: Wiley, 1968, chap. 12.

——— "Performance Evaluation in Marketing Systems." *Management Science*, July 1964.

——— *Quantitative Analysis for Marketing Management*. New York: McGraw-Hill, 1967, chap. 5.

[13] For a discussion of these various approaches, see William R. King, *Quantitative Analysis for Marketing Management* (New York: McGraw-Hill, 1967) chap. 5.

———— and Cleland, David I. "Manager-Analyst Teamwork in MIS Design." *Business Horizons,* April 1971.

———— and Wilson, T. A. "Subjective Time Estimates in Critical Path Planning—A Preliminary Analysis." *Management Science* 13 (January 1967).

McCarthy, J., and Hayes, P. "Some Philosophical Problems from the Standpoint of Artificial Intelligence." In D. Michie and B. Meltzer, eds., *Machine Intelligence 4.* Scotland, Edinburgh University Press, 1969.

Morton, M. *Management Decision Systems.* Division of Research, Graduate School of Business Administration. Cambridge, Mass.: Harvard University, 1971.

Murdick, R. G. and Ross, J. E. "Future Management Information Systems: Part I." *Journal of Systems Management,* April 1972, pp. 22–25.

————. "Future Management Information Systems: Part II." *Journal of Systems Management,* May 1972, pp. 32–35.

Nilsson, J. J. *Problem-Solving Methods in Artificial Intelligence.* New York: McGraw-Hill, 1971, chap. 6.

Peirce, C. S. "Ampliative Reasoning." In *Collected Papers of C. S. Peirce,* vol. II. Cambridge, Mass.: Harvard University Press (Belknap Press), chap. 5.

Pople, H., and Werner, G. "An Information Processing Approach to Theory Formation in Biomedical Research." *AFIPS Conference Proceedings* 40. Spring Joint Computer Conference, May 1972.

Robinson, J. A. "A Review of Automatic Theorem Proving." *Proc. Symp. Appl. Math* 19. American Math Society, 1967.

Thompson, H. *Joint Man/Machine Decisions.* Systems and Procedures Association, Cleveland, Ohio, 1965.

Appendix

Projects for Student Teams

Project 1

The following is a set of objectives and strategies which have been defined by a bank to guide its operations.* You, as the MMIS design team, have pulled these together from various sources and established their credibility.

1. Use these objectives and policies to establish a preliminary set of each of the following:
   a. *Objectives* for an MMIS
   b. Specifications of *MMIS characteristics*
   c. *Constraints* on the MMIS design
   d. *Design and development principles* which will be used in the MMIS design and development project
2. Since these objectives and strategies have been developed during a preliminary study phase for the MMIS, you will also have the opportunity to identify other information which your team would like to have in order to completely develop an MMIS project proposal.

Statement of Bank Objectives and Strategies

For individual and commercial customers and prospects

   a. Accessible, flexible facilities for deposit and receipt of cash checks, bonds, drafts, and other negotiable documents
   b. Interest-paying system to encourage time deposits
   c. Safekeeping facilities for valuable records
   d. Personal, confidential, knowledgeable consultation on all financial matters

For loan customers and prospects

   a. Facilities and experienced personnel available for consultation and financial advice on all loan matters

* Adapted with permission from *IBM Study Organization Plan: Documentation Techniques,* Manual C20-8075, 1961.

b. Readily accessible facilities for the closing of (and payment of) personal, commercial, or mortgage loans
c. Extensive advertising program to attract loan prospects to the bank for consultation
d. Specialist available with a broad knowledge of income-producing investments
e. Specialists available having detailed information on financial status of local individuals and businesses
f. Analysts available who are well informed on relative valuations of all types of property
g. Flexible interest-charging structure to encourage large loans and rewards for those who pay when due

Planned strategies to meet objectives

a. Expand advertising program to reach more potential customers.
b. Enlarge number of drive-up banking facilities.
c. Increase emphasis on installment-type loans.
d. Modernize and reorganize physical and manpower facilities as necessary for most efficient operation.
e. Develop services and systems to facilitate achievement of objectives with view in mind of offering these services to local businesses on a fee basis.

Project 2

The U.S. Department of Defense was faced in early 1973 with the problem of marketing military services for the first time in modern history. Since the early 1940s, the selective service system, or draft, had provided personnel to fulfill military requirements. With the end of the draft came the substantial task of maintaining an establishment of over two million peacetime military personnel while being prepared for fulfilling significantly larger requirements in the event of national emergency.

Military planners, who had not previously thought of themselves as marketers, were abruptly placed in the position of thinking in marketing terms and of developing an effective MMIS to support their decisions. Place yourself in this position and try to conceptualize an entirely new marketing problem, to develop a marketing strategy, to assess informational needs, and finally to conceptualize the general design for an MMIS.

In doing this, you should consider the unique opportunities that you may have for affecting the demand for new recruits, the market segments that you would identify, the various "products" that you might wish to differentially promote in appealing to various market segments, the nature of the marketing appeals that you might use, and the other marketing variables which you may be able to control in this unique situation.

After you have conceptualized the problem, spell out the information requirements which would permit you to make rational choices in each of the marketing areas. You might define these in terms of a series of questions which need to be answered before you could develop a strategy.

Once your informational questions are specified, lay out a schematic diagram of the MMIS that you might wish to have. This diagram should relate information, information sources, and information uses in a form that would facilitate the more detailed development of a system.

In performing this task you should think of yourself as the sole decision maker and ignore the organizational dimension. This simplification is necessary because of the great variety and complex undefined relationships which actually existed in the Department of Defense when this new marketing problem was initially faced.

Index